Microsoft® Excel for Accounting

MANAGERIAL AND COST

Katherine T. Smith, D.B.A.
Business Consultant

L. Murphy Smith, D.B.A., CPA
Texas A&M University

Lawrence C. Smith, Jr., Ph.D.
Louisiana Tech University

Pearson
Education

UPPER SADDLE RIVER, NEW JERSEY 07458

Acquisitions Editor: Alana Bradley
Editor-in-Chief: P. J. Boardman
Editorial Assistant: Jane Avery
Program Consultant: Walter Mendez
Executive Marketing Manager: Beth Toland
Managing Editor (Production): John Roberts
Permissions Coordinator: Suzanne Grappi
Associate Director, Manufacturing: Vincent Scelta
Production Manager: Arnold Vila
Manufacturing Buyer: Michelle Klein
Cover Design: Kiwi Design
Printer/Binder: Victor Graphics

Pearson Education LTD.
Pearson Education Australia PTY, Limited
Pearson Education Singapore, Pte. Ltd
Pearson Education North Asia Ltd
Pearson Education, Canada, Ltd
Pearson Educación de Mexico, S.A. de C.V.
Pearson Education–Japan
Pearson Education Malaysia, Pte. Ltd

10 9 8 7 6 5 4 3
ISBN 0-13-008553-7

DEDICATION

To the students who use this book. We hope each of you will enjoy the true success which is measured by moral character and personal integrity. Solomon said, "A good name is more desirable than great riches; to be esteemed is better than silver or gold."

To our beloved children: Jacob, Tracy, and Hannah. "Children are a gift from God; they are His reward" (Psalm 127:3). You are treasures from heaven.

To our parents: Genita and Hubert Taken, and Doris and Junior Smith.

KTS & LMS

To Doris Elaine Barfoot Smith, my beautiful wife. To Chris, Snook, Patti, Doug, and Angie. You've blessed my life.

LCS

CONTENTS

PREFACE

The purpose of this book is to introduce students to the fundamental tools and techniques available in Microsoft Excel™ spreadsheet software. Applications are presented that pertain to specific managerial and cost accounting topics. Students will learn through experience by following directions and creating the example worksheets shown in each chapter. Assignments may be selected from those contained within the book or other sources provided by your instructor.

The book provides detailed instructions for using Microsoft Excel. These instructions are designed for the most current version of Excel but are applicable for most other versions as well. Additional information is available on the website corresponding to this book.

WEBSITE

For updates, example files, suggested assignment schedules, and other helpful information, check the website (http://www.IOLBV.com/murphy/EXCEL4AcctMANA).

ACKNOWLEDGMENTS

The authors are grateful for the contributions to this project made by Michelle Chandler, Alana Bradley, and Kristi Shuey. We are thankful to Chris Osborne for regular doses of spiritual inspiration. Additionally, the authors appreciate the support and encouragement they have received, over the years, from the following colleagues:

Craig Bain, Northern Arizona University
Alan Blankley, University of North Carolina at Charlotte
James Flagg, Texas A&M University
Danny Ivancevich, University of North Carolina at Wilmington
Susan Ivancevich, University of North Carolina at Wilmington
David Kerr, Texas A&M University
Jeff Miller, Augusta State University
Steve McDuffie, Southwest Missouri State University
Uday Murthy, University of South Florida
Alan Sangster, University of Aberdeen
Bob Strawser, Texas A&M University
Jim Thompson, Oklahoma City University
Chris Wolfe, Texas A&M University

About the Authors

Katherine Taken Smith

Dr. Katherine T. Smith has served on the faculties at the University of Mississippi and Louisiana Tech University. Dr. Smith has authored numerous research articles which have appeared in various professional journals such as *The CPA Journal, Today's CPA, Accounting Education* (UK), and *National Public Accountant*. Currently she serves on the editorial boards of five national journals. She has authored seven books, including an educational novel entitled *The Bottom Line is Betrayal* (http://www.iolbv.com/murphy/novels/) which has been described as an "instructional thriller" that provides an innovative way to present business concepts and issues to students. In addition, she has made presentations at professional meetings in the U.S. and abroad.

L. Murphy Smith

Dr. L. Murphy Smith, CPA is Assistant Department Head and Professor in the Accounting Department at Texas A&M University. He received his doctorate from Louisiana Tech University. Dr. Smith's accomplishments include over 200 professional journal articles, research grants, books, and professional meeting presentations in the U.S. and abroad. His major research interests are systems, auditing, ethics, and international issues. His work has been cited in various news media, including *Fortune, USA Today*, and *The Wall Street Journal*. Among the books he has published, his accounting information systems text (http://acct.tamu.edu/smith/books/aisbook/) is now in its third edition. He serves on the editorial boards of several journals, including *Advances in International Accounting, Journal of Information Systems, Research on Accounting Ethics, Teaching Business Ethics*, and *The CPA Journal*.

Lawrence C. Smith, Jr.

Lawrence C. Smith, Jr., PhD is a Professor of Economics at Louisiana Tech University. He received his doctorate from the University of Mississippi. He has developed expertise on a wide variety of business and economics issues. In his distinguished career, Dr. Smith has made significant academic contributions in teaching, research, and service. He has played many roles in various professional organizations, including serving 27 years as Secretary-Treasurer of the Academy of Economics and Finance. In 1999 he was selected as the first Fellow of the Academy of Economics and Finance. Dr. Smith's accomplishments include numerous professional journal articles, books, and professional meeting presentations. Among the journals in which he has published are the following: *Journal of Economic Education, Journal of Economics and Finance, Southwestern Economic Review, Journal of Real Estate Appraisal and Economics*, and Oil, Gas & Energy Quarterly.

Computer Basics 1

This chapter briefly describes components of the personal computer, operating systems software, Windows, and starting your spreadsheet program.

COMPONENTS OF THE COMPUTER

As shown in Exhibit 1.1, the basic personal computer system consists of a monitor, keyboard, and a central processing unit (CPU). The CPU consists of three components: main memory, arithmetic logic unit, and supervisory control. Main memory includes random access memory (RAM) and read-only memory (ROM). The RAM of a typical personal computer may be as little as 640 kilobytes (K) or as much as 256 megabytes (MB).

The box or chassis containing the CPU also contains other devices such as the graphics card which connects to the monitor, a parallel port which connects to a printer, a serial port which connects to a mouse, a modem which connects to the phone line, a hard disk drive which provides secondary storage (typically ranging from four to 100 gigabytes), a floppy disk drive, and a CD-ROM or CD-RW drive. Another increasingly common feature on personal computers is a network card (e.g. ethernet) which enables a computer to be connected to a local area network or intranet, which then permits access to the Internet and the World Wide Web. The most widely used floppy disk drive is the 3.5 inch high density (HD) drive. The 3.5 inch HD disk can store 1.44 megabytes (MB) of data. A CD-ROM or CD-RW can store up to 640 MB of data.

The keyboard on your computer is made up of three basic sections: the function keys, the numeric key pad, and the alphanumeric keys. The alphanumeric keys, the main part of the keyboard, include letters, numbers, and a variety of symbols. The function keys, labeled F1 through F12, have different uses depending on the software currently in use.

The numeric pad is located on the right side of your keyboard. A significant key on the numeric pad is the NUM LOCK key, which is a toggle key that enables the user to switch between the number keys and the cursor control keys located on the numeric pad.

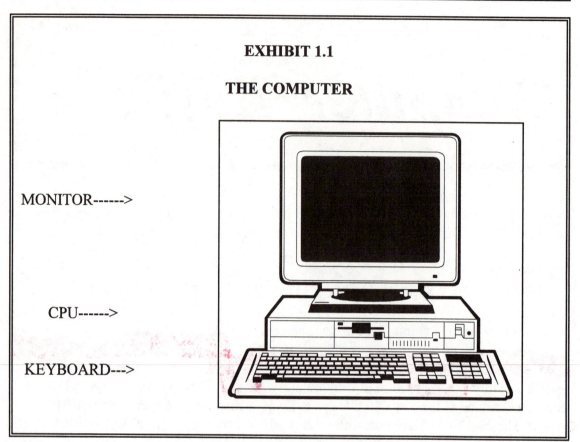

EXHIBIT 1.1

THE COMPUTER

MONITOR------>

CPU------>

KEYBOARD--->

OPERATING SYSTEMS SOFTWARE

An operating system runs your computer and manages your computer's activities. The operating system of the personal computer functions much like the operating systems on the mainframe or minicomputer. For the IBM-compatible system, the most popular operating system is Microsoft's Windows. The Apple Macintosh has an operating system called System 7.

Windows is a set of software programs that provides a graphical user interface. When running Windows, the computer user interacts with the computer visually and by use of a mouse rather than typing commands. New versions of Windows are typically released with much fanfare. Windows XP was introduced in New York City to a backdrop of a gospel choir singing "America the Beautiful," followed by pop star Sting performing a free concert in Bryant Park.

WINDOWS OPERATING SYSTEM

The most prominent feature of Windows is the use of icons (little pictures) to represent programs or groups of programs. After Windows is loaded (running), you run programs such as Excel by moving the pointer to the icon and double-clicking the left mouse button. A program icon represents a "shortcut" in Windows. Programs can also be accessed via the "start" button on the lower menu-bar. By clicking on "Start," you are given various options such as Run, Find, Settings, and Programs.

Microsoft periodically upgrades its Windows program. The current release is Windows XP. In Windows, "folders" and "shortcuts" refer to directories and executable programs. A folder may contain several shortcuts (which access specific programs such as Excel or Lotus 1-2-3). Each folder has a menu bar which allows creation of shortcuts or folders within that folder (select "File"-"New").

LOADING YOUR EXCEL SPREADSHEET PROGRAM

Excel by Microsoft Corporation is the most widely used spreadsheet software. To start Excel, follow these steps:

1. In Windows, use your mouse to click on the "Start" button on the bottom left side of your computer screen. The button should expand into a box with several options for selection.

2. From the Start menu, select the Programs options, which will open another box with options. If Microsoft Excel is listed separately, double-click the Excel option to open (run) the program. If there is not a separate listing for Microsoft Excel, then scroll to the Microsoft Office option and select Microsoft Excel.

OR

*   If an Excel icon is shown on the screen, double-click on that icon.

BASIC COMMANDS

SAVING A FILE

A worksheet is saved like any other file by using the following commands:

1.   Choose "File" in the menu bar and select the Save-As option.
2.   The Save-As menu box will appear and the name "Book1.xls" will be highlighted in the file name box. "Book1" is simply the default name which Excel uses and "xls" is the filename extension of an Excel worksheet. You can replace "Book1" with a new filename; we recommend keeping the "xls" extension so that your file will be recognized as an Excel worksheet.
3.   Now that you have named the worksheet, you can save it in the future by simply clicking on the Save icon (picture of a floppy disk).

CLOSING FILES

Similar to other files, a worksheet is closed by simply clicking on the "X" button in the upper right-hand corner of the menu bar on your worksheet.

RETRIEVING FILES

A worksheet is retrieved like any file by using the following commands:

1.   Click on the "Open" icon (picture of an open folder).
2.   An Open File box will appear with a list of files or folders. Double-click on the file you want opened. Note: If the file is not listed, then you are in the wrong folder. Access the correct folder by clicking on the arrow next to the "Looking in" box at the top. A list of folders or directories will appear for your choosing. Alternatively, you can search for a file with Windows Explorer program (using "Tools - Find").

EXITING

The Excel program can be exited like any other program by clicking on the "X" button in the upper right-hand corner of the screen (this appears above the "X" button used for closing the worksheet).

Making a Worksheet 2

WORKSHEET LAYOUT

Once the spreadsheet software is loaded, a screen appears similar to Exhibit 2.1. A spreadsheet file is often referred to as a worksheet.

EXHIBIT 2.1
BASIC EXCEL WORKSHEET

The letters across the top of a worksheet correspond to columns. The numbers along the left side of a worksheet correspond to rows. The box at the intersection of a column and row is referred to as the cell location. Cells are where data, either text or mathematical expressions, are entered. In Exhibit 2.1, the words "Cell A1" have been typed into cell A1. Directly above the cell is the control panel which shows the cell designation, in this case it is A1. To the right of that, next to an equal sign, you'll notice another panel containing "Cell A1." When a cell is clicked upon, its contents automatically appear in this panel.

Each Excel file, called a workbook, can hold several worksheets. Worksheets are saved, closed and printed like any other file, by clicking on the "File" selection in the top menu bar or by clicking on the appropriate icons.

AN ILLUSTRATION

To begin your familiarization with Excel worksheets, we will create a worksheet using just the essential commands. Step-by-step instructions to accomplish these commands will be provided.

Assume that you work in the accounting department at a local grocery store. Your boss has requested a breakdown of sales by department, comparing the last two years. To accomplish this, we'll create a worksheet with the data contained in the example worksheet shown in Exhibit 2.2. To begin, click on cell A1 with your mouse and type in "Sales." When finished typing, press Enter or click on another cell; the typed data will automatically be inserted into the worksheet. Now click on cell A3 and type in "Produce." Another way to move among the cells is to use the arrow keys. Proceed to type in the remaining data so that your worksheet looks like Exhibit 2.2. Column B is left empty simply for the purpose of improving the appearance of the worksheet.

EXHIBIT 2.2
GROCERY STORE WORKSHEET

	A	B	C	D	E
1	Sales				
2			12/31/x1	12/31/x2	
3	Produce		300	350	
4	Bakery		100	150	
5	Florist		50	20	
6	Deli		225	290	
7	Meat		550	600	
8	Dairy		410	500	
9					
10					

Note that Excel automatically right-justifies a number after it is entered into a cell. If you make a mistake in typing the numbers, the ensuing section on editing will reveal how to correct it.

EDITING

A cell can be put into edit mode by double clicking on the cell. Excel will then allow you to move around within the cell and change the contents. If you want to replace the entire contents of a cell, simply click on the cell once and type in the new contents. If you want to delete the entire contents of a cell, click on the cell and press the delete key.

As noted earlier, when a cell is clicked upon, its contents automatically enter the panel at the top of the worksheet next to the equal sign (=). Another way to edit a cell is to place your cursor within this panel and type.

If you make a mistake using any of the following commands, you can undo it by clicking on the "undo" icon (an arrow curving backwards).

MOVING CELL CONTENTS

Perhaps our worksheet would look better if "Sales" was placed more in the center of the worksheet. To move "Sales" to cell C1:

1. Click on the cell you wish to move (A1).
2. Position your cursor anywhere along the border of the cell until the cursor turns into a white arrow. Hold down the left mouse button and drag the arrow to the new cell. Release the mouse button, and the contents will appear in the new cell.

To move a block of cells, highlight the cells by holding down the left mouse button and then move the entire block at once. Cells can also be moved by using the "copy and paste" commands (discussed later in the chapter).

INSERTING ROWS AND COLUMNS

Suppose you decide that the worksheet would look better with a space between the title and the date headings. You want to insert a blank row between "Sales" on row 1 and the dates on row 2. The row can be inserted as follows:

1. Rows are added **above** the cell pointer, so position your cell pointer accordingly. In our example, click on any cell in row 2.
2. Click on "Insert" in the menu bar and choose "Rows" to insert.

Suppose you want to insert a column between the years (columns C and D). Columns are added to the **left** of the pointer, so to add the column in our example, click on any cell in column D. Click on "Insert" in the menu bar and choose "Columns." Exhibit 2.3 shows the new format with a blank row 2 and the sales figures in columns C and E.

EXHIBIT 2.3
GROCERY STORE WORKSHEET

	A	B	C	D	E
1			Sales		
2					
3			12/31/x1		12/31/x2
4	Produce		300		350
5	Bakery		100		150
6	Florist		50		20
7	Deli		225		290
8	Meat		550		600
9	Dairy		410		500
10					
11					

DELETING AND SHIFTING CELLS

Assume that the Florist department was discontinued at our store last month and should not be in the worksheet. As previously discussed, the contents of a cell can be removed by clicking on the cell and pressing the delete key. However, we want the florist data removed without leaving a row of empty cells. This is accomplished by deleting the unwanted row and shifting the remaining rows up. Regarding our grocery store worksheet, use the following commands:

1. Click on the cell which contains "Florist."
2. Click on "Edit" in the menu bar and choose the Delete option.
3. Excel gives you the option of deleting the entire row; click on that option. The rows below the deleted row will be shifted up.

If we had not chosen the option of deleting the entire row, than only the cell containing "florist" would have been deleted and only the cells within column A would have been shifted up. If an entire column is deleted, columns will be shifted to the left.

CENTERING

Data within a single cell can be centered by clicking on the cell and then clicking on the icon which displays centered lines. The icon is found on the top toolbar, just to the right of the bold (**B**), italicize (*I*), and underline (U) icons. Center each of the dates in the worksheet. Multiple cells may be centered at the same time by first highlighting the range of cells and then clicking on the icon.

Suppose we need a different heading on the worksheet. Delete "Sales." In the same cell, type "Grocery Store Sales by Department." The heading will run over into the adjacent empty cells. Press enter to leave the edit mode. To center the new heading between columns A and E, first highlight row 1 from A to E. Then click on the icon with the boxed-in "a" (merge and center icon) at the top of the tool bar. Exhibit 2.4 shows the new heading.

CHANGING COLUMN OR ROW WIDTH

When the spreadsheet program is first loaded, the column width will be eight characters. If your cell data exceeds the cell width, the data will simply run into the adjacent empty cell. However, if the adjacent cell is not empty, the overflow data will be truncated at the cell border. To avoid this, column width can be changed. Using our example worksheet, type the heading "Total Sales Per Year" into cell A9. To accommodate the long heading, widen column A using the following instructions. Note: It is best to be out of the edit mode when changing cell width; click on a blank cell to exit the edit mode.

1. Position the cursor at the top of the screen on the mid-point between the lettered column headings (i.e., between A and B). The cursor should change into a "+."
2. Click-and-drag using the left mouse key; hold it while "dragging" the column to a different width.

Your worksheet should now resemble Exhibit 2.4. (We will total the sales per year in Chapter 3 using a special Excel command.) Row width can be changed by positioning the cursor between the row numbers on the left side of the worksheet.

COPY AND PASTE

The "copy and paste" commands enable you to duplicate the contents of one or more cells to other locations on the worksheet. Anything already in the receiving cell will be deleted. To copy and paste, highlight the cell(s) to be copied, click on the copy icon, then move the cursor to the desired location and click the paste icon. If you want to delete the cell contents from the original location, you can use the cut and paste icons or the commands which are accessed via "Edit" on the menu bar.

EXHIBIT 2.4
GROCERY STORE WORKSHEET

	A	B	C	D	E
1	Grocery Store Sales by Department				
2					
3			12/31/x1		12/31/x2
4	Produce		300		350
5	Bakery		100		150
6	Deli		225		290
7	Meat		550		600
8	Dairy		410		500
9	Total Sales Per Year				
10					
11					

Special paste commands can be accessed by clicking on "Edit" in the menu bar and choosing the "Paste Special" option. Here are two useful "paste special" commands which can be used on cells or entire worksheets.

1. The "Microsoft Excel Worksheet" option allows you to paste a worksheet into a document (e.g. a Word file) and then activate Excel by simply clicking on the worksheet in your document.

2. The "Picture" option pastes the worksheet contents without the gridlines. The grocery store worksheet was pasted into Exhibit 2.5 using the Picture option.

EXHIBIT 2.5
WORKSHEET PASTED USING "PICTURE" OPTION

Grocery Store Sales by Department

	12/31/x1	12/31/x2
Produce	300	350
Bakery	100	150
Deli	225	290
Meat	550	600
Dairy	410	500
Total Sales Per Year		

PRINTING

For printing your worksheet, it is helpful to first highlight the section you want printed and then click on "File" in the menu bar. Select "Print." Under the print options, choose "Selection." Another very useful step is to select "File - Print Preview" to see how your output will look. By skipping these steps, and depending on where the cursor is, you could print several pages unnecessarily. Occasionally, you may need to designate the range of cells to be printed. To do so, highlight the range to be printed (e.g. A1 to H40) and then click on File - Print Area - Set Print Area.

Formulas, Functions, and Formatting 3

This chapter presents Excel features which are especially useful for manipulating numbers within accounting related worksheets. The features include automatic sums, formulas, functions, and numeric formatting.

The Grocery Store worksheet that was created in Chapter 2 will also be used in this chapter as an example. If you do not still have the worksheet on your computer, recreate it as shown in Exhibit 3.1

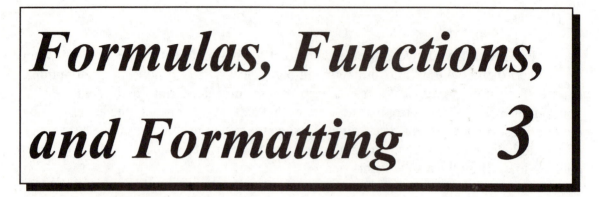

EXHIBIT 3.1
GROCERY STORE WORKSHEET

	A	B	C	D	E
1	Grocery Store Sales by Department				
2					
3			12/31/x1		12/31/x2
4	Bakery		100		150
5	Deli		225		290
6	Produce		300		350
7	Dairy		410		500
8	Meat		550		600
9	Total Sales Per Year				
10					

AUTOMATIC SUMS

Excel contains an icon with the Greek sigma sign (Σ). This icon is called "Autosum" and will automatically sum numbers within the cells you select. Using the example worksheet, total each year's sales using the following instructions:

1.   Highlight the cells to be summed (for year 1: cells C4 through C8).

2.   Click on the Autosum button. The total will automatically be inserted into the next lower cell (C9).

In the latest version of Excel, the Autosum icon is accompanied by a down arrow. Upon clicking on the arrow, other functions will be displayed, such as averaging numbers and counting cells.

Note: If a number has more characters than a cell will hold, the number signs (####) will appear. To correct this, simply widen the column or decrease the font size.

Repeat the Autosum process for the second year's column. To enhance the appearance of the worksheet, place a line under the figures being summed (i.e., cells C8 and E8). To place an underscore in a cell, click on the appropriate cell and then click on the underscore icon (U). Your worksheet should now resemble Exhibit 3.2.

EXHIBIT 3.2
GROCERY STORE WORKSHEET

	A	B	C	D	E
1	Grocery Store Sales by Department				
2					
3			12/31/x1		12/31/x2
4	Bakery		100		150
5	Deli		225		290
6	Produce		300		350
7	Dairy		410		500
8	Meat		550		600
9	Total Sales Per Year		1585		1890

FORMULAS

WRITING FORMULAS

Formulas can be used to manipulate numeric data. They are entered just as they would be processed algebraically. For example, to add the contents of cells C9 and E9, the following steps are necessary:

1.   In the cell in which you want the result to appear, type the formula:
=C9+E9
2.   Press "Enter" to place the results of the equation in the cell.

The same process applies to subtraction, division, and multiplication. The multiplication symbol is the asterisk (*). The division symbol is the slash (/).

Note: When an equal sign is the very first thing entered, Excel knows it is a mathematical expression. If there is a space before the equal sign, Excel will read it as text.

COPYING FORMULAS

We will use our grocery store worksheet to practice writing and copying formulas. Suppose the boss wants a column which shows how much sales have increased or decreased between the two years. Type the heading "Difference" into cell D3. Next, in cell D4, type the formula: =E4-C4. Press "Enter."

Instead of entering the formula into multiple cells, you can copy this formula into the other cells. The cell addresses will automatically adjust as you copy a formula from one cell to another. If a formula is copied down the length of a column, the address will change corresponding to the row in which the formula is placed. Copy the formula into the other cells in your worksheet by:

1.   Click on the cell which contains the formula (D4). Put the cursor on the small box in the bottom right corner of the cell (the fill handle); the cursor will turn to a "+".

2.   Drag the cell over the range of cells you want to fill (D5 through D9).

When the formula was copied into cell D5, the formula automatically changed from "=E4-C4" to "=E5-C5." This is referred to as **relative addressing**. Relative addressing occurs for both rows and columns.

Your worksheet should now resemble Exhibit 3.3. In the newest version of Excel, an Autofill options box pops up; it can be ignored. Autofill will be discussed in Chapter 5.

The alternative to relative addressing is called **absolute addressing**. This means that the cell references do not adjust, but they remain exactly as they were in the source cell of the copy procedure. To make a formula absolute you must precede that portion of the formula with a dollar sign ($). Thus, if you want to copy a formula such as =C2*D5 and you want to make C2 an absolute address, you would type the formula as =C2*D5 before copying.

EXHIBIT 3.3
GROCERY STORE WORKSHEET

	A	B	C	D	E
1	Grocery Store Sales by Department				
2					
3			12/31/x1	Difference	12/31/x2
4	Bakery		100	50	150
5	Deli		225	65	290
6	Produce		300	50	350
7	Dairy		410	90	500
8	Meat		550	50	600
9	Total Sales Per Year		1585	305	1890
10					

FUNCTIONS

Functions are basically pre-written formulas. They save time and increase accuracy. We will create a new worksheet to practice using functions. Remember that a workbook can contain several worksheets. If you want to add a new worksheet to an existing workbook file, simply click on the tab at the bottom entitled "Sheet2." If you prefer an new workbook file, one can be created by clicking on the icon of a blank white sheet of paper found on the upper-left of the tool bar.

Assume that you are asked to prepare a worksheet to calculate loan payments based on the information below. Type the data from Exhibit 3.4 into a new worksheet. Note that column A will need to be widened to accommodate the words "annual payments." Review: To widen a column, position the cursor on the mid-point between the lettered column headings. When the cursor changes into a "+," click-and-drag the column width.

EXHIBIT 3.4
LOAN PAYMENTS WORKSHEET

	A	B	C	D
1	Rate	0.1	0.05	0.06
2	Years	10	20	8
3	Principal	100000	30000	20000
4	Annual Payments			

To calculate the annual payments for our example loan payments worksheet, the use of the @PMT function is explained below.

1. Click on the cell in which you want the annual payment to appear (B4).
2. Click on the "fx" icon which represents the Functions Wizard.
3. Choose Financial under the Functions category box.
4. Choose PMT under the Function name box. Then click OK.
5. Enter the cell locations which contain the rate, nper, and pv. Use the mouse to click on the different boxes.
    In this example, rate is B1. Nper (years) is B2. Pv (principal) is B3. (The formula is =PMT(rate, nper, pv). Excel will also ask for fv and type; leave those blank. Click on OK.

Note: If a cell is not wide enough to accommodate a number, then you will see "######" in the cell. Simply widen the column and the correct number ($16,274.54) will appear. Excel automatically formats the loan payment in dollars.

Do not use the Functions Wizard to calculate the remaining annual payments; instead we will save time by copying the formula into the other cells. Review on how to copy a formula: Click on the cell which contains the formula (B4). Put the cursor on the small box in the bottom right corner of the cell; the cursor will turn to a "+". Drag the cell over the range of cells you want to fill (C4 and D4).

Exhibit 3.5 includes the annual loan payment calculations.

EXHIBIT 3.5
LOAN PAYMENTS WORKSHEET

	A	B	C	D
1	Rate	0.1	0.05	0.06
2	Years	10	20	8
3	Principal	100000	30000	20000
4	Annual Payment	($16,274.54)	($2,407.28)	($3,220.72)

DATE AND OTHER FUNCTIONS

The Functions Wizard of Excel has many useful functions available in addition to those that perform basic arithmetic. For example, by typing "=today( )" into a cell, the worksheet will always show the actual date. If you typed a particular date into the parentheses, the worksheet would always show that date. Other functions and their symbols are described in Exhibit 3.6.

EXHIBIT 3.6
EXCEL FUNCTIONS

SYMBOL   DESCRIPTION

Financial Functions:

FV	Returns the future value of an investment.
IPMT	Returns the interest payment for an investment for a given period.
IRR	Returns the internal rate of return for a series of cash flows.
NPV	Returns the net present value of an investment based on a series of periodic cash flows and a discount rate.
PMT	Returns period payments for an annuity.
PV	Returns the present value of an investment.
RATE	Returns the interest rate per period of an annuity.

Date and Time Functions:

DATE	Returns the serial number of a particular date.
DAY	Converts a serial number to a particular day of the month.
DAYS360	Calculates the number of days between two dates based on a 360-day year.
TIMEVALUE	Converts the time in the form of text to a serial number.
TODAY	Returns the serial number of today's date.

Math and Trig Functions:

COUNTIF	Returns the number of nonblank cells in a given range which meet the given criteria.
INT	Rounds a number down to the nearest integer.
ROUND	Rounds a number to the specified number of digits.
SUBTOTAL	Returns a subtotal in a list or database.
SUM	Adds the specified numbers.

Statistical Functions:

AVERAGE	Returns the average of the specified numbers
COUNT	Counts how many numbers are in a given range.
MAX	Returns the maximum number in a specified range.
MEDIAN	Returns the median of the specified numbers.
MIN	Returns the minimum number in a specified range.
MODE	Returns the most common value in a specified range.

NUMERIC FORMATTING

Using our example loans payment worksheet, we will format the numbers in a simple manner using the tool bar icons. Customized formatting using the menu bar will also be discussed.

PERCENTAGE SYMBOL

The icon of a percentage symbol (%) automatically converts numbers to percentages. In your worksheet, select the cells which contain values for Rate (B1 through D1) and click on the percentage icon. If your software doesn't have the percentage icon, click on "Format - Cells" in the menu bar and then select "Number - Percentage." Exhibit 3.7 shows the percentages.

CURRENCY STYLE

The icon of a dollar sign ($) is called "currency style" and will automatically add a dollar sign, decimal, and cents places to any cell you select. In your worksheet, select the cells which contain values for Principal and click on the dollar icon. Alternatively, click on "Format - Cells" in the top menu bar and then select "Number - Currency."

If you accidentally insert a currency style into the wrong cell, you must go to the Format menu to un-format the cell. Click on "Format" in the menu bar and choose "Cells." Under the Number tab choose "Currency." Excel will offer several options, scroll till you select "None" for symbols and "0" for the number of decimal places. Variations in currency formats are described in the Customized Formatting section.

Your worksheet should now resemble Exhibit 3.7.

EXHIBIT 3.7
LOAN PAYMENTS WORKSHEET

	A	B	C	D
1	Rate	10%	5%	6%
2	Years	10	20	8
3	Principal	$ 100,000.00	$ 30,000.00	$ 20,000.00
4	Annual Payment	($16,274.54)	($2,407.28)	($3,220.72)

COMMAS

The icon of a comma automatically inserts commas into the appropriate places. The columns will automatically widen to accommodate the numerical formatting.

CUSTOMIZED FORMATTING

If you need a format other than what the icons provide, you can customize the formatting of a cell through the menu bar by using the following instructions.

1. Highlight the cells to be formatted.
2. Click on Format in the menu bar and select "Cells."
3. Choose the category and options you desire.

Exhibit 3.8 displays some of the variations in numeric formatting.

EXHIBIT 3.8
EXAMPLES OF AVAILABLE NUMERIC FORMATS

Format Type	Display
Number	1234 1,234.00 (any number of decimal places may be chosen) -1,234.56 (negative number can also be in parenthesis or in red)
Date	3/14 3/14/98 March - 98 March 14, 1998 3/14/98 1:30 PM Some options have the time displayed along with the date.
Time	13:30 1:30 PM 13:30:55
Percentage	5% or 5.00% (any number of decimal places may be chosen)
Currency	$1,234 $1,234.00 (any number of decimal places may be chosen) $(1,234.56) negative number
Special	Numbers can be formatted as zip codes, phone numbers, or social security numbers.

Charts

4

The spreadsheet program allows you to create charts or graphs as a way to visually represent numeric data. Excel refers to both charts and graphs as simply "charts." Before creating a chart, the data which is to be used in the chart must be typed into a worksheet. Next, you highlight the data and click on the Chart Wizard icon (a bar chart with blue, yellow, and red columns). The Chart Wizard will guide you through a four step process for creating a chart. A chart is linked to the worksheet data and is automatically updated when the data in the worksheet is changed. The following sections give specific directions on creating different types of charts.

First, set up a new worksheet containing the data in Exhibit 4.1; this data will be used for each of the following charts. Assume that you work for a company which has sales in the United States, Europe, and Asia.

EXHIBIT 4.1
SALES WORKSHEET

	A	B	C	D	E	F
1	SALES BY YEAR AND BY REGION					
2						
3		USA	Europe	Asia	Total Sales	
4	2002	534	231	69		
5	2001	518	146	71		
6	2000	427	75	44		
7	1999	405	239	22		
8	1998	267	119	36		
9	1997	188	84	25		
10						

Use the Autosum icon to total the sales for each year. Review: Highlight the row containing the first year's sales (cells B4 through D4). Click on Autosum and the total will automatically be entered into the next cell (E4). Remember to save time by copying the formula (cell E4) into the remaining cells (cells E5 to E9). Review: Click on the cell which contains the formula (E4). Put the cursor on the small box in the bottom right corner of the cell; the cursor will turn to a "+". Drag the cell over the range of cells you want to fill.

In the latest version of Excel, a green triangle may appear which indicates that a message corresponds to that cell. In this case, Excel is notifying us that the formula did not sum all of the cells in the row (we intentionally did not include the cell containing the year).

COLUMN CHART

A column chart, like a line chart, is a one-dimensional chart. Assume your boss wants to see a comparison of each region's sales over the past six years. You decide to use a column chart. First, highlight the data range which contains the information that will be plotted, in this case that would be the columns containing the years and each region's sales, including their titles (i.e., cells A3 through D9). The headings are being included so that Chart Wizard can use them in the chart legend. Next, click on the Chart Wizard icon. It will present the following four steps:

Step 1.   Select a specific chart type. For this example, select Column chart. Then you will be able to choose from several chart sub-types. Choose the first sub-type box which is labeled "clustered column." Click on "Next."

Step 2.   In this step, Chart Wizard is confirming the data range which you previously highlighted and the fact that your data is in columns. There is a display showing what your chart currently looks like. Click on "Next."
Note: By default, Chart Wizard plots whatever there is fewer of - rows or columns - as the data series. Since our example has fewer columns, the columns containing sales figures were automatically plotted as data series. Chart Wizard uses the first column as the x-axis IF it does not have a heading AND the remaining columns do. Thus, the column containing the years was automatically used for the x-axis instead of being plotted as another data series.

Step 3.   Several chart enhancing options are made available here. Type a title into the title box. Type "Year" into the x-axis box and "Sales" into the y-axis box. These are the only selections necessary for this example. Click on "Next."

Step 4.   Chart Wizard places the chart into your current worksheet unless you select the option of placing it into a new sheet. Click "Finish" and your chart will appear on your worksheet.

When completed, your column chart should resemble Exhibit 4.2. The chart can be repositioned on the worksheet by clicking on it and dragging it to a new position. The chart box can be enlarged by clicking and expanding its borders like any other box.

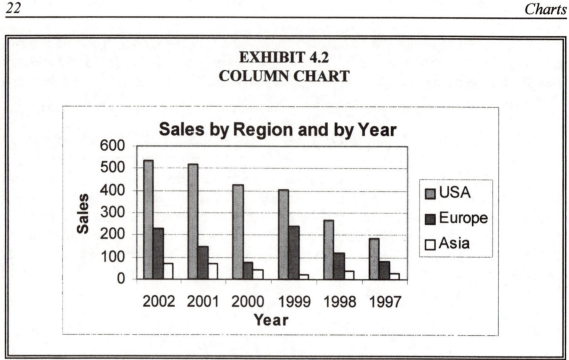

EXHIBIT 4.2
COLUMN CHART

Sales by Region and by Year

To print a chart, highlight it and select "Print" or "Print-preview." Print-preview allows you to first make setup changes such as size and page orientation (portrait or landscape). To delete a chart from your worksheet, simply click on the chart and press the Delete key.

STACKED-COLUMN CHART

A stacked-column chart is one variation of a column chart. Instead of placing bars next to each other, it stacks shaded bars for multiple ranges of data on top of each other. Try charting the same data range using the stacked-column chart. Click on the Chart Wizard icon and follow the four step process previously described. After selecting the column chart type, we chose the second chart sub-type labeled "stacked column." Your chart should resemble the stacked-column chart in Exhibit 4.3.

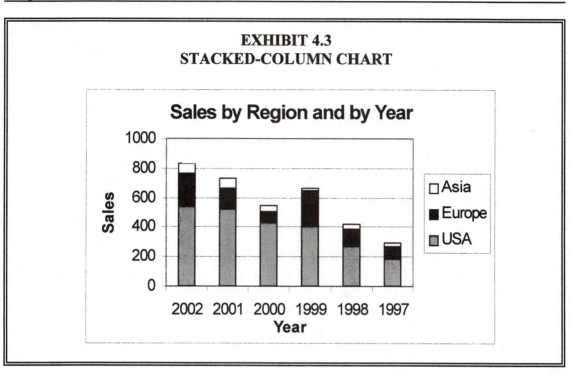

EXHIBIT 4.3
STACKED-COLUMN CHART

LINE CHART

A line chart is used for plotting data on a vertical y-axis and a horizontal x-axis. The y-axis can contain from one to six ranges, producing one to six lines.

Suppose the boss wants to see the total sales trend over the past six years. You decide to use a line chart. The same four step process using Chart Wizard will be used, but this time we will describe some additional options. Highlighting the data range needed for the chart is a bit more difficult since the Total Sales column is not lined up next to the years in the worksheet. We could move the columns around on the worksheet, but instead we will select the x-axis values through the Chart Wizard process. First, highlight the Total Sales column (cells E3 through E9). Next, click on Chart Wizard.

Step 1. Select the Line chart option. For the sub-type, we chose the first box in the second row which is labeled "Line with markers displayed." Click on "Next."

Step 2. Chart Wizard is confirming our data range. There is a tab titled "Series," click on that tab. You'll see that Total Sales is listed as a data series. (If we had not highlighted the heading, it simply would be labeled Series 1. You could rename the data series at this point by typing a name into the "Name" box.)

At the bottom of the menu box, you'll see that the x-axis has not been designated. Click on the empty box beside "category (X) axis labels" and then, while still in Chart Wizard, highlight the years on your worksheet (cells A4 to A9). The range address will automatically be inserted into the box. Click on "Next."

Step 3.   Type in a chart title and axis labels. Click on the tab at the top marked "Data Labels." You are given options as to how to label the plotted line(s). Click on the option "show value." The sales values will appear on your chart. Chart Wizard will automatically show a chart legend unless you turn the option off in this step. Click on "Next."

Step 4.   Chart Wizard places the chart into your current worksheet unless you select the option of placing it into a new sheet. If you choose a new sheet, you can access the different sheets by clicking on the tabs at the bottom of the worksheet.

Exhibit 4.4 contains the line chart just created.

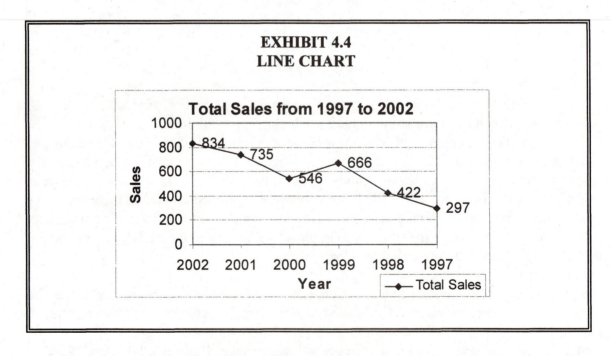

EXHIBIT 4.4
LINE CHART

After you have created the chart, changes can be made to the style of its various parts by right-clicking on the specific part and choosing to re-format. For example, the following changes were made to the chart in Exhibit 4.4.

•   The background area of the chart was changed to white by right-clicking on the chart area and accessing the Format Plot Area menu box. Several colors and border styles are made available.

- The style of the plotted lines can be modified by right clicking on the line and accessing the Format Data Series. The style and color of the line can then be changed.

- Excel automatically positions the category labels (Years) between the tick marks on the x-axis and thus plots the values between the tick marks. You can change this and create a direct alignment by right-clicking on the category axis (x-axis) and bringing up the Format Axis menu box, as shown in Exhibit 4.5. Next, click on the "Scale" tab and un-check the box next to "Value (Y) axis crosses between categories."

EXHIBIT 4.5
FORMAT AXIS MENU BOX - SCALE TAB

Format Axis   ? ✕

| Patterns | Scale | Font | Number | Alignment |

Category (X) axis scale

Value (Y) axis crosses
   at category number: [1]

Number of categories
   between tick-mark labels: [2]

Number of categories
   between tick marks: [1]

☐ Value (Y) axis crosses between categories
☐ Categories in reverse order
☐ Value (Y) axis crosses at maximum category

[OK]   [Cancel]

PIE CHART

A pie chart can be used to graph only a single range of data (i.e., one column or one row of values). For this example, we'll chart the sales for the year 2002 only. First, highlight the **row** containing the 2002 sales data, and include the row containing the regional titles (cells B3 through D4). Click on Chart Wizard and follow the four step process. Under pie chart, we selected the second sub-type choice labeled "pie with a 3-D visual effect." In step 3, we chose to use percentages and names as data labels for the pie slices by changing the settings found under the "Data Labels" tab. Under the "Legend" tab, we deleted the legend by clicking on and thus removing the check mark in the "Show Legend" box.

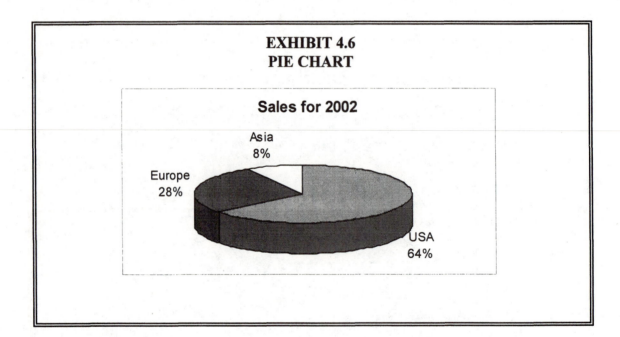

EXHIBIT 4.6
PIE CHART

Sales for 2002

Asia
8%

Europe
28%

USA
64%

Worksheet Manipulation 5

RANGE NAMES

Sometimes keeping track of the cell addresses to be included in a range can be quite tedious. Excel provides a command to name ranges and thus refer to the cell addresses by that name. Using range names is useful in sorting, formatting, copying, and printing.

We'll use the sales worksheet from Chapter 4 to practice creating a range name. The worksheet is shown in Exhibit 5.1. Suppose you frequently print the USA's sales figures and, thus, it would save time to use a range name instead of always highlighting the cells.

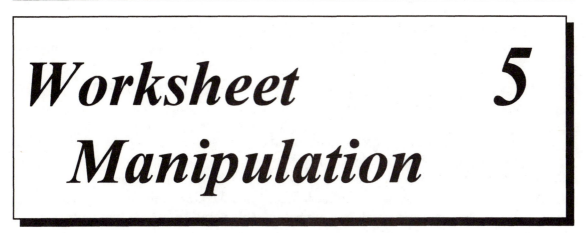

EXHIBIT 5.1
SALES WORKSHEET

	A	B	C	D	E
1	SALES BY YEAR AND BY REGION				
2					
3		USA	Europe	Asia	**Total Sales**
4	**2002**	534	231	69	834
5	**2001**	518	146	71	735
6	**2000**	427	75	44	546
7	**1999**	405	239	22	666
8	**1998**	267	119	36	422
9	**1997**	188	84	25	297

Create a range name for the USA column by following these steps:

1. Highlight the cells that you want to name as a range (B3 through B9). (Note: If you include the title when you initially highlight the range,

Excel will automatically insert the title as the range name.)
2.   Click on "Insert" in the menu bar and select the Name option. Then select "Define."
3.   The name you selected will appear, or you can type in a new name. Click on "OK."

Click on a blank cell to remove the highlighting. Now click on the arrow within the cell designation panel, also called the "name box" (the box directly above column A). As shown in Exhibit 5.2, this will reveal any ranges which have been named. Click on the "USA" range name which you just created; this causes the USA column to be highlighted. Once a range name has been created, you may use this name anywhere that requires a cell address.

EXHIBIT 5.2
CELL DESIGNATION PANEL

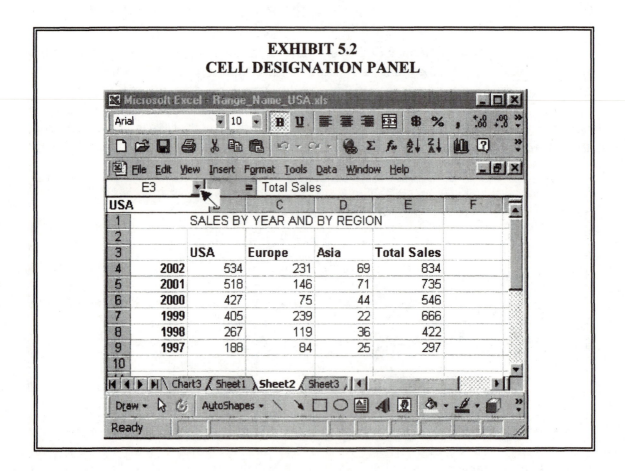

		USA	Europe	Asia	Total Sales
	1	SALES BY YEAR AND BY REGION			
	2				
	3	USA	Europe	Asia	Total Sales
	4	2002	534	231	69	834
	5	2001	518	146	71	735
	6	2000	427	75	44	546
	7	1999	405	239	22	666
	8	1998	267	119	36	422
	9	1997	188	84	25	297
	10				

FREEZE PANES

When working on a large worksheet, sometimes the entire worksheet does not fit on the screen. The Freeze Panes command allows you to freeze rows or columns. The cells on one side of the freeze line remain stationary, while the cells on the other side of the line can be scrolled. For example, a row of headings can be frozen while you scroll and view the remainder of the worksheet. Exhibit 5.3 illustrates freezing row 3 of our example worksheet; note that row 3 has remained at the top of the display, while the remaining worksheet has been scrolled to row 9.

EXHIBIT 5.3
FREEZE PANES

	A	B	C	D	E	F
1		SALES BY YEAR AND REGION				
2						
3		USA	Europe	Asia	Total Sales	
9	1997	188	84	25	297	
10						

The Freeze Panes command allows you to compare any rows or columns of data which are not already adjacent on the worksheet.

To use the Freeze Panes option, perform the following steps:

1. Click on the cell where you want the freeze to be. (For our example, A4.)
   a. For a **horizontal** freeze, the rows **above** the cell will be frozen. Click on the first cell of the row.
   b. For a **vertical** freeze, the columns to the **left** of the cell will be frozen. Click on the first cell of the column.
2. Click on "Window" in the menu bar and select the Freeze Panes option.

If you do not click on the first cell in the row or column, then you will achieve horizontal and vertical splits simultaneously. To remove the freeze, click on "Window" and select the Unfreeze Panes option.

SPLIT SCREEN

Under "Window" in the menu bar, there is an option called "Split." This is very similar to freezing panes. The only difference is that the part of the worksheet chosen to remain constant can also be duplicated on the screen by scrolling past it. (The freeze panes option does not duplicate the constant part of the worksheet.) To create a split screen, follow the directions for freeze panes except chose "Split" instead of "Freeze Panes."

IMPORTING DATA

Using the Clipboard feature, you are able to copy or "import" data from other spreadsheets or programs into your Microsoft Excel worksheet.

1. Open the file which contains the data you want imported into your Excel worksheet. Highlight the data that you want copied and copy it to the Clipboard by clicking on the copy icon (2 sheets of paper).

2. Select the area on the Excel worksheet to where the information should be imported and click on the Paste icon (clipboard).

Database Tools   **6**

Excel has several features which improve the ease of manipulating data in a worksheet. This chapter specifically covers data form, data sort, Autofill, and Autofilter.

Excel provides a database function which allows you to assimilate and manipulate related information. A **database** consists of **records** which contain **fields.** Fields are items such as an account title, an account number, or amount. Fields are made up of alphabetic characters (e.g. account title) or numbers (e.g. amount). Fields that are related are grouped together in records. For example, an accounts receivable record typically includes a field for account number, customer name, and balance. All the accounts receivable records comprise the database (customarily referred to as the accounts receivable master file).

Prepare a new worksheet with the data contained in Exhibit 6.1 using the following Excel feature called "data form."

DATA FORM

The purpose of data form is to reduce errors resulting from entering data into the wrong cell. When using data form, you provide Excel with the titles you want on the worksheet and it inserts these titles into a simplified form. You can then add information record by record. To duplicate the example worksheet using data form, perform the following steps:

1. Type the titles (i.e., account, name, balance, past due) into your worksheet. Refer to Exhibit 6.1 for the exact placement.
2. Highlight the titles. Click on "Data" in the menu bar and choose the "Form" option. You will be asked if the top row of your selection is the header row. Click on "OK."
3. An input box will automatically appear with your titles as the field names to the left of the input fields in the box. You can now begin entering data from your records. IMPORTANT: Use the TAB key when moving from one field to the next. After inserting all the data for one person (a record), press the Enter key.

Notes: Column B will need to be widened to accommodate the names. At this time, leave the "Account" field blank. When all the records are entered, click on Close. When you are finished, your worksheet should resemble Exhibit 6.1.

EXHIBIT 6.1
EXAMPLE ACCOUNTS WORKSHEET

	A	B	C	D	E
1	Account	Name	Balance	Past Due	
2		Miller, Rob	600	80	
3		Smith, John	220	20	
4		Jackson, Al	50	10	
5		King, James	200	60	
6		Brown, Amy	100	90	
7		Jones, Sara	145	40	
8					

DATA SORT

SORTING A SINGLE COLUMN OR ROW

Excel will sort numbers or words in an ascending or descending manner. The "sort ascending" icon displays the letter A on top of the letter Z; it will sort a list going from A to Z. The "sort descending" icon displays the letter Z on top of the letter A. A column can be sorted by simply clicking on any cell within the column and then clicking on the sort icon. Excel will prioritize alphabetic sorting over numeric sorting.

SORTING MULTIPLE COLUMNS OR ROWS

Suppose the boss wants to view the accounts receivable past due from shortest time past due to longest time past due. In this case, multiple columns need to be sorted in order to keep each person's record intact. Sorting is a bit more entailed since we want to sort by a specific column of numbers (past due amounts). Using your example worksheet, perform the following steps:

1.   Highlight each record (i.e., cells B2 through D7).
2.   Click on Data in the menu bar and choose "sort." Select the column by which you want the list sorted (past due). Excel gives you the option to sort ascending or descending; choose ascending.

Exhibit 6.2 shows the records by past due values in ascending order.

EXHIBIT 6.2
EXAMPLE ACCOUNTS WORKSHEET

	A	B	C	D
1	Account	Name	Balance	Past Due
2		Jackson, Al	50	10
3		Smith, John	220	20
4		Jones, Sara	145	40
5		King, James	200	60
6		Miller, Rob	600	80
7		Brown, Amy	100	90
8				

Now we will sort the worksheet in a different way using the data sort icon. Suppose the boss wants the list of names alphabetized in the worksheet. Again, to keep each person's record intact, multiple columns need to be sorted. Since Excel will prioritize alphabetic sorting over numeric sorting, it will automatically sort by the Names column (we do not need to specify a column). To alphabetize the records, performing the following steps:

1. Highlight the appropriate cells (B2 through D7).
2. Click on the "sort ascending" icon (picture of the letter A on top of the letter Z, with a down arrow along side of it).

Exhibit 6.3 shows the records alphabetized in ascending order.

EXHIBIT 6.3
RESULTS OF DATA SORT

	A	B	C	D
1	Account	Name	Balance	Past Due
2		Brown, Amy	100	90
3		Jackson, Al	50	10
4		Jones, Sara	145	40
5		King, James	200	60
6		Miller, Rob	600	80
7		Smith, John	220	20
8				

AUTOFILL

This command enables the user to fill a specified range with a sequence of numbers or text. Suppose you want to create a consecutive numbering system for customer account numbers, beginning with account number 1001 up to account number 1006. Perform the following steps:

1.   Type the first two values of the series (i.e., 1001, 1002) into the first two cells of your list. (Refer to Exhibit 6.4.)
2.   Highlight the two cells. Put the cursor on the small box in the bottom right corner of the cell (the fill handle); the cursor will turn to a "+".
3.   Drag the cell over the range of cells you want to fill. Release the mouse and AutoFill will automatically fill in the series of cells.

The result of this procedure is displayed in Exhibit 6.4.

EXHIBIT 6.4
RESULTS OF AUTOFILL

	A	B	C	D
1	Account	Name	Balance	Past Due
2	1001	Brown, Amy	100	90
3	1002	Jackson, Al	50	10
4	1003	Jones, Sara	145	40
5	1004	King, James	200	60
6	1005	Miller, Rob	600	80
7	1006	Smith, John	220	20
8				

AUTOFILTER

This command permits the user to select and view records in a database which meet a specific criterion set forth by the user. You determine your criteria by selecting what data from which fields you want to keep. For example, you may choose to view only those records for people who are 40 days or more past due. AutoFilter will allow you to do this by performing the following steps:

1.   Highlight all of the records including the titles.

2.   Click on "Data" in the menu bar. Choose the Filter option and then the AutoFilter.

3.   Small boxes with down arrows will appear in each cell containing a field title. These drop boxes will list options when the arrow is clicked.

4.   In order to view only those records that are 40 days or more past due, click on the down arrow in the Past Due cell. Several options will appear, choose the Custom option. (If you selected one of the numbers displayed, than only those records containing that number would be shown.)

5.   In the Custom AutoFilter menu box, click on the arrow within the first box in order to view your options. Select the "is greater than or equal to" option. Then, click on the next box to the right and type in "40." Click the OK button.

Your worksheet should now display only those records that are 40 days or more past due, as shown in Exhibit 6.5. To delete the AutoFilter, once again click on Data, then Filter, and uncheck the AutoFilter option by clicking on it.

EXHIBIT 6.5
RESULTS OF AUTOFILTER

	A	B	C	D
1	Acct	Name	Balance	Past Du
2	1001	Brown	100	90
4	1003	Jones	145	40
5	1004	King	200	60
6	1005	Miller	600	80

Macro Commands 7

Macros are shortcuts which allow you to reduce a series of different commands or keystrokes into a couple of simple clicks of the mouse. Microsoft Excel allows you to "record" the instruction of several commands and then replay or "run" the macro to activate the commands exactly as you performed them. Macros are efficient in performing time-consuming functions which are done frequently.

CREATING A MACRO

To illustrate the macro feature, we will use the example worksheet which was created in Chapter 6 and is shown below in Exhibit 7.1.

EXHIBIT 7.1
EXAMPLE ACCOUNTS WORKSHEET

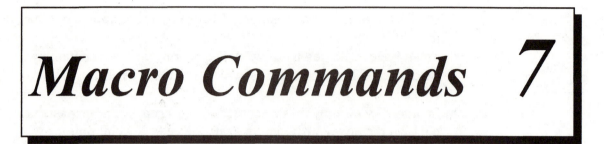

	A	B	C	D
1	Account	Name	Balance	Past Due
2	1001	Brown, Amy	100	90
3	1002	Jackson, Al	50	10
4	1003	Jones, Sara	145	40
5	1004	King, James	200	60
6	1005	Miller, Rob	600	80
7	1006	Smith, John	220	20
8				

Suppose the boss wants the accounts sorted according to each person's balance, going from largest to smallest. Since the account balances change often, let's create a macro that runs the sort procedure. The following steps describe how to create a simple macro, in this case, for sorting a worksheet.

1.   Turn on the macro recorder by clicking on "Tools" in the menu bar

and choosing the Macro option and then "Record New Macro."

2.   Enter a name for your macro in the Name box. You may replace the name Excel automatically inserted (Macro1) with a name of your choosing, such as "Sort." Click on "OK."

3.   A small box will appear on your worksheet labeled "Stop." The macro program will record every action you perform from now until the time you press the blue button in the box.

4.   Perform the task you want done. In this case, perform the sort feature: Highlight all the records, but not the titles (i.e., highlight cells A2 to D7). If the box is in the way, it can be moved by clicking on the title and moving the cursor. Click on "Data" in the menu bar and choose "Sort." In the Sort box, select the Balance column in descending order. Click on "OK."

5.   Click on the blue button in the Stop box.

Your worksheet should now resemble Exhibit 7.2.

EXHIBIT 7.2
SORTED BY BALANCE USING A MACRO

	A	B	C	D
1	Account	Name	Balance	Past Due
2	1005	Miller, Rob	600	80
3	1006	Smith, John	220	20
4	1004	King, James	200	60
5	1003	Jones, Sara	145	40
6	1001	Brown, Amy	100	90
7	1002	Jackson, Al	50	10

RUNNING A MACRO

Let's make use of the macro we just created. Suppose the account balances have changed in the past week. John Smith reduced his balance down to $120 and James King reduced his balance down to $80. Insert these new figures into your worksheet. Now we'll resort the accounts using the macro. To run the macro, perform the following steps:

1.   Select "Tools" in the menu bar and choose the Macro option and then "Macros."

2.   Choose the macro program you want and click on "Run."

This sorting task was relatively simple, but it illustrates the potential that macros have in saving time on tasks that must be constantly repeated.

Guidelines for   *8*
Worksheet Design

The following general guidelines should be considered when designing a worksheet; each will be discussed within this chapter.

1. Outline worksheet requirements (i.e., input and output).
2. Create a file identification area.
3. Establish data input areas separate from output areas.
4. Enter data in rows or columns, but not both.
5. Use manual recalculation when working with extremely large files.
6. Create backup files.
7. Test the worksheet.

REQUIREMENTS OUTLINE

The first guideline in creating a worksheet is to outline the worksheet requirements. What input is necessary to solve the problem at hand? What output is required? These requirements should be determined before beginning work. For example, assume you are required to create a worksheet that projects income statements for the next two years based on a constant growth rate in sales revenue. In this case, the required input is the current sales amount, annual sales growth rate, cost of goods sold as a percentage of sales, and the fixed amount of operating expenses.

The output requirement would be projected income statements for the next two years.

FILE ID

A file identification area should be prepared at the top of the worksheet. Prepare a new worksheet with the following file identification information: the file name, the worksheet designer's name, the input required, the output generated, and the dates the file was created, modified, and last used. See Exhibit 8.1 for an illustration.

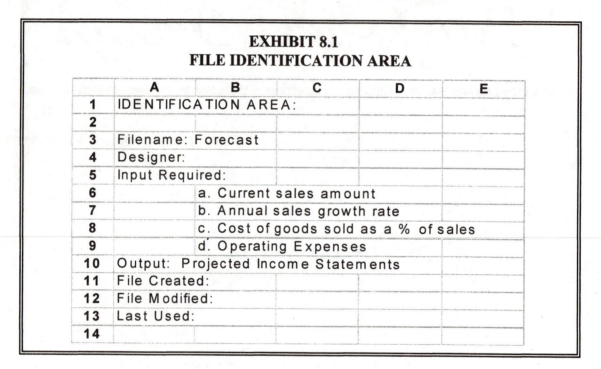

EXHIBIT 8.1
FILE IDENTIFICATION AREA

	A	B	C	D	E
1	IDENTIFICATION AREA:				
2					
3	Filename: Forecast				
4	Designer:				
5	Input Required:				
6		a. Current sales amount			
7		b. Annual sales growth rate			
8		c. Cost of goods sold as a % of sales			
9		d. Operating Expenses			
10	Output: Projected Income Statements				
11	File Created:				
12	File Modified:				
13	Last Used:				
14					

DATA INPUT

The data items necessary for using the worksheet are typed into one column of the input area. For this example, cost of goods sold is assumed to be a constant percentage of sales and operating expenses are assumed to be a fixed amount each year. The input area for our example worksheet is illustrated in Exhibit 8.2. Enter these input items along with their respective values into your worksheet. Be sure to put the values into column E. (We will be inserting formulas later with the cell address of E.)

Formulas within the output area are based upon values in the input area. This enables the user to modify any value in the input area and instantly see how the change affects the output.

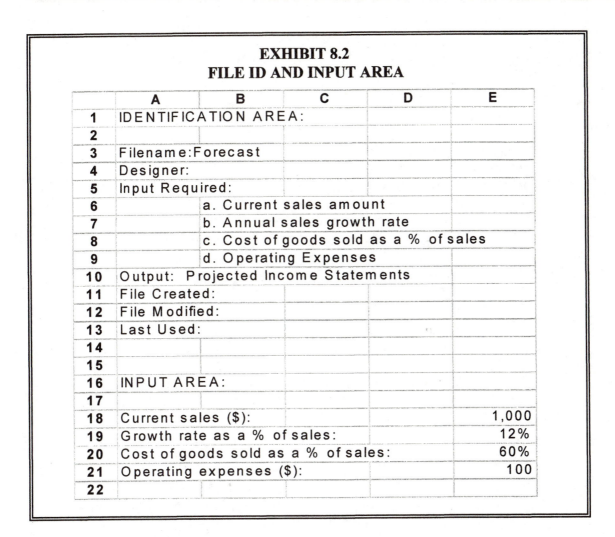

EXHIBIT 8.2
FILE ID AND INPUT AREA

	A	B	C	D	E
1	IDENTIFICATION AREA:				
2					
3	Filename:Forecast				
4	Designer:				
5	Input Required:				
6	a. Current sales amount				
7	b. Annual sales growth rate				
8	c. Cost of goods sold as a % of sales				
9	d. Operating Expenses				
10	Output: Projected Income Statements				
11	File Created:				
12	File Modified:				
13	Last Used:				
14					
15					
16	INPUT AREA:				
17					
18	Current sales ($):				1,000
19	Growth rate as a % of sales:				12%
20	Cost of goods sold as a % of sales:				60%
21	Operating expenses ($):				100
22					

DATA OUTPUT

The output area of the worksheet contains the desired results. The output for our example is projected income statements for the next two years. Exhibit 8.3 displays the output area items and formulas. Type these into your worksheet. For purposes of this example, the income statement is limited to only five line items. Exhibit 8.4 shows the computation results. Note: For uniformity, we formatted the income statements amounts to include two decimal places. This was easily accomplished by highlighting the appropriate cells and then clicking on the "increase decimal" icon (an arrow next to ".0"). Decimal places can also be specified by clicking on "Format" in the menu bar, as discussed in Chapter 3.

EXHIBIT 8.3
FILE ID, INPUT AND OUTPUT AREAS

	A	B	C	D	E
1	IDENTIFICATION AREA:				
2					
3	Filename:Forecast				
4	Designer:				
5	Input Required:				
6		a. Current sales amount			
7		b. Annual sales growth rate			
8		c. Cost of goods sold as a % of sales			
9		d. Operating Expenses			
10	Output: Projected Income Statements				
11	File Created:				
12	File Modified:				
13	Last Used:				
14					
15					
16	INPUT AREA:				
17					
18	Current sales ($):				1,000
19	Growth rate as a % of sales:				12%
20	Cost of goods sold as a % of sales:				60%
21	Operating expenses ($):				100
22					
23					
24	OUTPUT AREA:				
25					
26	Projected Income Statement for the Next Two Years				
27					
28				20x1	20x2
29					
30	Sales			=E18+E18*E19	=D30+D30*E19
31	Cost of goods sold			=D30*E20	=E30*E20
32					
33	Gross Profit			=D30-D31	=E30-E31
34	Operating Expenses			=E21	=E21
35					
36	Projected Net Income			=D33-D34	=E33-E34

EXHIBIT 8.4
OUTPUT AREA RESULTS

		20x1	20x2
24	OUTPUT AREA:		
25			
26	Projected Income Statement for the Next Two Years		
27			
28		20x1	20x2
29			
30	Sales	1120.00	1254.40
31	Cost of goods sold	672.00	752.64
32			
33	Gross Profit	448.00	501.76
34	Operating Expenses	100.00	100.00
35			
36	Projected Net Income	348.00	401.76

Once the output area is formatted by typing in the required items and formulas, the computations are totally formula driven, based upon values in the input area. As previously noted, this enables the user to modify any value in the input area and instantly see how the change affects the output. For example, change the growth rate percentage in the input area from 12% to 15%; you will instantly see the recalculations resulting in a net income of $360 for the first year and $429 for the second year.

INPUT ALIGNMENT

For maximum efficiency, the input cells should be aligned vertically (in a column) or horizontally (in a row), but not both. Fewer mistakes should occur if the user doesn't have to steer the cursor through a maze of input cells.

MANUAL RECALCULATION

If more than one value in the input area is to be changed on an extremely large worksheet, it is helpful to turn off Excel's automatic recalculation. This is because the software instantly recalculates mathematical expressions once a value has been modified. Data cannot be entered while the recalculations are taking place. The time involved is inconsequential for small worksheets but can become a burden for extremely large worksheets. A simple procedure is used to change from automatic recalculation to manual recalculation:

1.   Click on "Tools" in the menu bar and choose "Options."
2.   Select the Calculation tab.
3.   In the Calculation area, click on "Manual."

In the Manual mode, when a value in the input area is changed, the output values will not change in response. If you wish for Excel to recalculate an amount, without reinstating the automatic recalculation option, you can press the F9 key. Excel will recalculate for the values currently in the worksheet. When using manual recalculation, a good idea is to type a note on the worksheet that you must press "F9" to recalculate.

BACKUP FILES

Backup copies should be continually updated and stored in more than one place. When creating a worksheet, the user should periodically (every 15 to 30 minutes) save the file in case of a power outage or other event that may cause erasure of the file and the loss of hours of work.

TESTING

Any new worksheet should be manually tested. If formulas are involved, the user must test the worksheet result against an example that is already proven correct.

Step-by-Step Excel Example   9

This chapter provides step-by-step instructions for creating a simple worksheet and graph using Microsoft Excel spreadsheet software.

CREATING AN EXCEL WORKSHEET

Open a new worksheet and enter the information shown in Exhibit 9.1. Brief reviews of some of the Excel features are given if you should need them. Note that the sales amount of 1000 dollars must be placed in cell C6.

EXHIBIT 9.1
EXAMPLE WORKSHEET

	A	B	C	D	E	F
1	IDENTIFICATION AREA:					
2	Filename: Example					
3	Designer:					
4						
5	INPUT AREA:					
6	Sales in $ =		1000			
7						
8	OUTPUT AREA:					
9		JACOB & SISTERS BRICK COMPANY				
10		INCOME STATEMENT				
11		For the Year Ended December 31, 20x1				
12						
13	Sales					
14	Cost of sales					
15	Gross profit					
16	Operating expense					
17	Net Income					
18						

EDITING A CELL

A cell can be put into edit mode by double clicking on the cell. Excel will then allow you to move around within the cell and change the contents. After you have finished the edit typing, press "Enter" to insert the contents into the worksheet. If you want to delete the entire contents of a cell, click on the cell and press the delete key.

CENTERING

After the company name and income statement headings are typed in, they are centered by highlighting each row individually from A to E (e.g. A9 to E9) and then clicking on the centering icon (the boxed-in letter "a" between arrows pointing left and right) at the top of the tool bar.

INSERTING FORMULAS

Formulas are entered just as they would be processed algebraically, using cell addresses to represent values in the equation. When an equal sign is the very first symbol entered, Excel knows this cell contains a mathematical expression. (If there is a space before the equal sign, Excel will read it as text.)

Assume that the company expects sales of $1,000 for the year ended 12/31/x1. The cost of sales is expected to be 60 percent of sales and operating expenses average 10 percent of sales. Using this information, we can create formulas for each of the items on our worksheet. Type the formulas from Exhibit 9.2 into your worksheet; press "Enter" after each entry.

EXHIBIT 9.2
FORMULAS FOR EXAMPLE WORKSHEET

	A	B	C	D	E
8	OUTPUT AREA:				
9	JACOB & SISTERS BRICK COMPANY				
10	INCOME STATEMENT				
11	For the Year Ended December 31, 20x1				
12					
13	Sales		=C6		
14	Cost of sales		=C13*.60		
15	Gross profit		=C13-C14		
16	Operating expense		=C13*.10		
17	Net Income		=C15-C16		

Your worksheet should now contain the correct values for each item, as shown in Exhibit 9.3

EXHIBIT 9.3
EXAMPLE WORKSHEET - OUTPUT

8	OUTPUT AREA:			
9	JACOB & SISTERS BRICK COMPANY			
10	INCOME STATEMENT			
11	For the Year Ended December 31, 20x1			
12				
13	Sales	1000		
14	Cost of sales	600		
15	Gross profit	400		
16	Operating expense	100		
17	Net Income	300		
18				

MANIPULATING DATA

The worksheet just created can be used for any amount of sales by simply changing the value for sales in the input area. The computations in the output area are totally formula driven, based on amounts in the input area. This enables the user to modify any value in the input area and instantly see how the change affects the output. For example, change the value of sales from $1000 to $2000 in the input area; click on cell C6 and type in 2000. You'll note that each item in the output area was automatically recalculated and the new net income is $600.

NUMERIC FORMATTING

If you wish to include dollar signs and commas, click on the cells containing currency. Once the cells are selected, click on the icon of a dollar sign ($). Alternatively, you can click on "Format" in the menu bar and then select "Cells - Number - Currency."

COLUMN EXPANSION

When the spreadsheet program is first loaded, the column width will be eight characters. If your cell data exceeds the cell width, the data will simply run into the adjacent empty cell; this is what occurred in our example worksheet. However, if the adjacent cell is not empty, the overflow data will be truncated at the cell border. To avoid this, column width can be changed using the following steps. Note: It is best to be out of the edit mode when changing cell width; click on a blank cell to exit the edit mode.

1. Position the cursor at the top of the screen on the mid-point between the lettered column headings (i.e., between A and B). The cursor should change into a "+."
2. Click-and-drag using the left mouse key; hold it while "dragging" the column to a different width.

PRINTING

For printing your worksheet, it is helpful to first highlight the section you want printed and then click on "File" in the menu bar. Select "Print." Under the print options, choose "Selection." Another very useful step is to select "File - Print Preview" to see how your output will look. By skipping these steps, and depending on where the cursor is, you could print several pages unnecessarily.

CREATING AN EXCEL PIE CHART

Before creating a chart, the data which is to be used in the chart must be typed into a worksheet. Next, you highlight the data and click on the Chart Wizard icon (picture of blue, yellow, and red columns on a bar chart). The Chart Wizard will guide you through a four step process for creating a chart. A chart is linked to the worksheet data it's created from and is automatically updated when the data in the worksheet is changed

We'll prepare a pie chart of the division of sales revenue using Chart Wizard. A pie chart can be used to graph only a single range of data (i.e., one column or one row of values). Use the values corresponding with sales of $2000. Skip down a couple of lines on your worksheet and type in the data as shown in Exhibit 9.4.

EXHIBIT 9.4
SCHEDULE OF DATA FOR PIE CHART

	A	B	C
20	Cost of sales		1200
21	Operating expense		200
22	Net Income		600

Highlight the data range which contains the information that will be charted (C20 to C22). Next, click on the Chart Wizard icon. It will present the following four steps:

Step 1.   Select a specific chart type. For this example, select Pie chart. Then you will be able to choose from several chart sub-types. Choose the first sub-type box which is labeled "Pie." Click on "Next."

Step 2.   In this step, Chart Wizard is confirming the data range which you previously highlighted and the fact that your data is in columns. There is a display showing what your chart currently looks like. There is a tab titled "Series," click on that tab. Here, we can insert labels for our pie slices. Click on the empty box next to "Category Labels" at the bottom. Then, while still in Chart Wizard, highlight the labels on your worksheet (cells A20 to A22 containing the words "cost of sales, operating expense, net income"). The range address will automatically be inserted into the box. Click on "Next."

Step 3.   Several chart enhancing options are made available here. Type a title into the title box. Under the Data Labels tab, we choose "show percent." Click on "Next."

Step 4.   Chart Wizard places the chart into your current worksheet unless you select the option of placing it into a new sheet. Click "Finish" and your chart will appear on your worksheet.

Your pie chart should resemble Exhibit 9.5. The chart can be repositioned on the worksheet by clicking on it and dragging it to a new position. The chart box can be enlarged by clicking and expanding its borders like any other box.

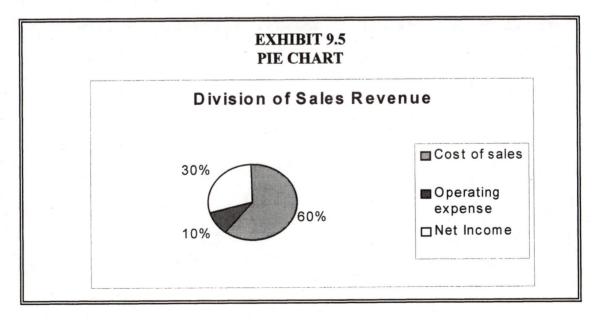

EXHIBIT 9.5
PIE CHART

Division of Sales Revenue

30%   10%   60%

☐ Cost of sales
■ Operating expense
☐ Net Income

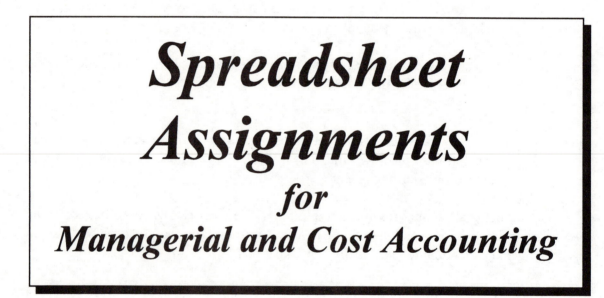

Spreadsheet Assignments
for
Managerial and Cost Accounting

LIST
of Spreadsheet Assignments

The list below provides a brief description of each assignment and related accounting topic area. Solutions to selected assignments are shown at the end of the book. In addition, a number of example worksheet files are available on the book's website (IOLBV.com/murphy/EXCEL4AcctMANA).

ACCOUNTING TOPIC	No.	DESCRIPTION
Introduction to Managerial Accounting	1	Cost of Goods Manufactured and Cost of Goods Sold
	2	Income Statement
Analyzing Cost Behavior	3*	Cost-Volume-Profit Analysis
	4	Cost-Volume-Profit Analysis
Job Order Costing	5	Work in Process and Questions
Process Costing	6	Compute Equivalent Units: FIFO
	7*	Compute Equivalent Units: Weighted Average
Overhead Costs and Activity Based Costing	8	Cost Allocation Rates
	9	Budgeted Costs, ABC Cost Per Unit
	10	Manufacturing Cost Based on ABC Unit Cost
Cost-Volume-Profit Analysis	11	Cost-Volume-Profit Analysis
	12	Cost-Volume-Profit Analysis
	13	Cost-Volume-Profit Analysis: Graph
	14*	Cost-Volume-Profit Analysis: Graph
	15	Graph Cost Behavior Patterns
	16	Contribution Margin Income Statement
Costs	17	Departmental Income Statement

---

* Indicates that the solution to the assignment is at the end of this book.

ACCOUNTING TOPIC	**No.**	**DESCRIPTION**
Budgeting	18	Flexible Budget
	19	Graph Total Cost Line
Use of Managerial Accounting Data	20	Product Mix Analysis
for Decision-Making	21	Make or Buy Analysis
Responsibility Accounting	22	Best Use of Facilities Analysis
Capital Budgeting	23	Flexible Budget
	24	Flexible Budget
Financial Statement Analysis	25	Financial Ratios
	26	Financial Ratios
	27	Common Size Balance Sheets
	28	Common Size Balance Sheets
	29	Horizontal Analysis of Income Statement
Statement of Cash Flows	30	Statement of Cash Flows
	31	Statement of Cash Flows
International Operations	32	Foreign Currency Translation Using the Current Rate Method
	33*	Foreign Currency Translation Using the Current Rate Method
	34	Foreign Currency Translation Using the Current Rate Method
	35	Foreign Currency Translation Using the Current Rate Method
	36	Foreign Currency Translation Using the Temporal Rate Method
	37	Foreign Currency Translation Using the Temporal Rate Method
	38	Economic Impact of an Import Quota
	39*	Economic Impact of an Import Quota
	40-42	Economic Impact of a Tariff
Case Problem		Starts on Page 80

---

* Indicates that the solution to the assignment is at the end of this book.

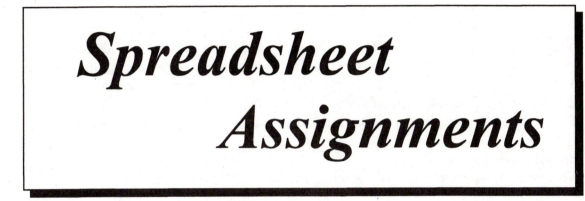

1.   COST OF GOODS MANUFACTURED AND COST OF GOODS SOLD

Prepare a schedule of cost of goods manufactured and a schedule of cost of goods sold from the following information. Use applied overhead in the schedule of cost of goods manufactured; the applied overhead rate is 50 percent of direct labor charges. In the schedule of cost of goods sold, show the adjustment for over/underapplied overhead. (Hint: overhead is underapplied in the amount of $3,000.)

	Beginning of Year	End of Year
Materials inventory	$22,000	$28,000
Work-in-process inventory	38,000	30,000
Finished-goods inventory	18,000	25,000
Purchases of raw materials		78,000
Direct labor		82,000
Indirect labor (overhead item)		15,000
Insurance on plant (overhead item)		9,000
Depreciation-plant building and equipment (overhead item)		16,000
Repairs and maintenance-plant (overhead item)		4,000
Marketing expenses		77,000
General and administrative expenses		29,000
Income tax expense		30,000

Optional What-if Scenario:
What is the impact of changing the beginning work in process from $38,000 to $45,000?

2.   INCOME STATEMENT

Prepare an income statement for XYZ Company. Assume that XYZ sold 27,000 units of its product at a price of $14 during the current year. Use the following additional information: (1) beginning finished goods inventory = $18,000; (2) cost of goods manufactured = $206,000; (3) ending finished goods inventory = $25,000; (4) marketing expenses = $77,000; (5) general and administrative expenses = $29,000; and (6) income taxes = $30,000.

Optional What-if Scenario:
What is the impact of changing the price from $14 to $16?

3.   COST-VOLUME-PROFIT ANALYSIS

Prepare a worksheet that illustrates cost-volume-profit (CVP) analysis, also referred to as break-even analysis. Use the following formulas:
     CMU = SPU - VCU
     Where: CMU is contribution margin per unit.
              SPU is sales price per unit.
              VCU is variable cost per unit.

     BEP (units) = TFC / CMU
     Where: TFC is total fixed cost.
              CMU is contribution margin per unit.

Assume that sales price per unit is $20; that variable cost per unit is $16; and that total fixed cost is $24,000. Calculate the contribution margin per unit, the break-even point in units of sales, and the break-even point in dollars of sales. In the input area, show sales price per unit, variable cost per unit, and total fixed cost. In the output area, show sales price per unit, variable cost per unit, contribution margin per unit, total fixed cost, breakeven point in units, and breakeven point in dollars.
Note: The solution to this problem is at the end of the book.

4.   COST-VOLUME-PROFIT ANALYSIS

Same as assignment 3 except that the sales price per unit is increased from $20 to $22.

5.   WORK-IN-PROCESS AND RELATED QUESTIONS

August production generated the following activity in the Work-in-Process Inventory account of Zumikazi Manufacturing Company:

Work in Process Inventory

August 1 Balance	10,000
Direct materials used	28,000
Direct labor charged to jobs	31,000
Manufacturing overhead allocated to jobs	11,000

Completed production, not yet recorded, consists of Jobs B-78, G-65, and Y- 11, with total costs of $16,000, $27,000, and $33,000, respectively.

A.   Compute the cost of work in process at August 31.
B.   Prepare the journal entry for production completed in August.
C.   Prepare the journal entry to record the sale (on credit) of Job G-65 for $41,000. Also make the cost-of-goods-sold entry.
D.   What is the gross margin on Job G-65? What other costs does this gross margin have to cover?

Optional What-if Scenario:
What is the impact of changing the cost of Job G-65 from $27,000 to $29,000?

6.   COMPUTE EQUIVALENT UNITS -- FIFO

Selected production and cost data of Harmon's Hardwood Flooring, follows for May 20X1:

	Flow of Physical Units	
Flow of Production	Sanding Department	Finishing Department
Units to account for:		
Beginning work in process, April 30	20,000	6,000
Transferred in during May	70,000	80,000
Total physical units to account for	90,000	86,000
Units accounted for:		
Completed and transferred out during May:		
From beginning inventory	20,000	6,000
Started and completed during May	60,000	75,000
Work-in-process, May 31	10,000	5,000
Total physical units accounted for	90,000	86,000

Harmon's uses FIFO process costing.

A.   Fill in the blanks:

   a.   On April 30, the Sanding Department beginning work-in-process inventory was 80% complete as to materials and 90% complete as to conversion costs. This means that for the beginning inventory, ___% of the materials and ___ % of the conversion costs were added during May.
   b.   On May 31, the Sanding Department ending work-in-process inventory was 60% complete as to materials and 40% complete as to conversion costs. This means that for the ending, inventory ___% of the materials and ___% of the conversion costs were added during May.
   c.   On April 30, the Finishing Department beginning work-in-process inventory was 33 1/3% complete as to materials and 60% complete as to conversion costs. This means that for the beginning inventory ___% of the materials and ___% of the conversion costs were added during May.
   d.   On May 31, the Finishing Department ending work-in-process inventory, was 70% complete as to materials and 60% complete as to Conversion costs. This means that for the ending inventory ___% of the materials and ___% of the conversion costs were added during May.

B.   Use the Flow of Production data and the information in requirement 1 to compute the equivalent units for transferred-in costs (if necessary), direct materials, and conversion costs for both the Sanding Department and the Finishing Department.

Optional What-if Scenario:
What is the impact of changing the following:
    Sanding-transferred-in from 70,000 to 80,000
    Sanding-started-and-completed from 60,000 to 70,000
    (Thus, total sanding units to account for is now 100,000)

7.   COMPUTE EQUIVALENT UNITS -- WEIGHTED AVERAGE

Repeat Requirement B from assignment 6 for the Finishing Department, using the weighted-average method. Note: The solution to this problem is at the end of the book.

Optional What-if Scenario:
What is the impact of changing the units transferred in from 80,000 to 70,000? (Thus total units to account for is now 76,000.)

8.   COST ALLOCATION RATES

Chromium Ltd. uses activity-based costing for its manufacturing process. Company managers have identified four manufacturing activities: materials handling, machine setup, insertion of parts, and finishing. The budgeted activity costs for 20X1 and their allocation bases are as follows:

Activity	Total Budgeted Cost	Allocation Base
Materials handling	$12,000	Number of parts
Machine setup	2,400	Number of setups
Insertion of parts	24,000	Number of parts
Finishing	60,000	Finishing direct labor-hours
Total	$98,400	

Chromium expects to produce 2,000 chrome wheels during the year. The wheels are expected to use 12,000 parts, require 6 setups, and consume 1,000 hours of finishing time.

A.   Compute the cost allocation rate for each activity.
B.   Compute the indirect manufacturing cost of each wheel.

Optional What-if Scenario:
What is the impact of changing the materials handling cost from $12,000 to $6,000?

9.   BUDGETED COSTS, ABC COST PER UNIT

Several years after reengineering its production process, Chromex hired a new controller, Rebecca Steinberg. She developed an ABC system very similar to the one used by Chromex's chief rival, Chromium, Ltd., described above. Part of the reason Steinberg developed the ABC system was that Chromex's profits had been declining, even though the company had shifted its product mix toward the product that had appeared most profitable under the old system. Before adopting the new ABC system, Chromex had used a direct labor hour single-allocation-base system that was developed 20 years ago.
For 20X1, Chromex's budgeted ABC allocation rates are:

Activity	Allocation Base	Cost Allocation Rate
Materials handling	Number of parts	$ 1.25 per part
Machine setup	Number of setups	300.00 per setup
Insertion of parts	Number of parts	3.00 per part
Finishing	Finishing direct labor-hours	70.00 per hour

The number of parts is now a feasible allocation base because Chromex recently purchased bar coding technology. Chromex produces two wheel models: standard and deluxe. Budgeted data for 20X1 are as follows:

	Standard	Deluxe
Parts per Unit	5.0	7.0
Setups Per 1,000 units	3.0	3.0
Finishing direct labor hours per unit	0.2	1.0
Total direct labor hours per unit	2.0	3.0

The company's managers expect to produce 1,000 units of each model during the year.

A. Compute the total budgeted cost for 20X1.
B. Compute the ABC cost per unit of each model.
C. Using Chromex's old direct labor hour single allocation-base system, compute the (single) allocation rate based on direct labor hours. Use this rate to determine the cost per wheel for each model under the old single-allocation-base method.

Optional What-if Scenario:
What is the impact of changing the materials handling allocation rate from $1.25 to $2.00?

10.   MANUFACTURING COST BASED ON ABC UNIT COST

For 20X2, Chromex's managers have determined the following conversion costs per wheel: ABC (indirect) cost per standard wheel is $36.15 and per deluxe wheel is $100.65; alternatively, single-rate (indirect) cost per standard wheel is $54.72 and per deluxe wheel is $82.08. In addition to the unit conversion costs, the following data are budgeted for the company's standard and deluxe models for 20X2:

	Standard	Deluxe
Sale price	$110.00	$155.00
Direct materials	15.00	25.00

Because of limited machine hour capacity, Chromex can produce either 2,000 standard wheels or 2,000 deluxe wheels.

A. If the managers rely on the ABC unit cost data, which model will they produce? Show support for your answer. (All non-manufacturing costs are the same for both models.)

B. If the managers rely on the single-allocation-base cost data, which model will they produce? Show support for your answer.

C. Which course of action will yield more income for Chromex? Show support for your answer.

Optional What-if Scenario:
What is the impact of changing the sales price of the standard model from $110 to $75?

11. COST-VOLUME-PROFIT ANALYSIS

Prepare a worksheet that illustrates cost-volume-profit (CVP) analysis, also referred to as break-even analysis. Use the following formulas:

CMU = SPU - VCU

Where:
CMU is contribution margin per unit.
SPU is sales price per unit.
VCU is variable cost per unit.

BEP (units) = TFC / CMU

Where:
TFC is total fixed cost.
CMU is contribution margin per unit.

Assume that sales price per unit is $10; that variable cost per unit is $8; and that total fixed cost is $24,000. Calculate the contribution margin per unit, the break-even point in units of sales, and the break-even point in dollars of sales.

12. COST-VOLUME-PROFIT ANALYSIS

Same as assignment 11 except that the sales price per unit is increased from $10 to $12.

13. COST-VOLUME-PROFIT ANALYSIS: GRAPH

Assume that sales price per unit is $12, variable cost per unit is $8, and total fixed cost is $24,000. Prepare a line graph to illustrate break-even analysis. To prepare the graph, first set up a table with columns for units, total fixed cost (TFC), total variable cost (TVC), total cost (TC), sales revenue, and profit. In the units column, show values from zero to 8,000, in increments of 1000. Graph the data in columns for total fixed cost, total cost, and sales revenue. The formula for a line is typically expressed as $y = a + bx$. Applying this to our three lines, the formulas could be expressed as follows:

TFC = $24,000 + $0 * units
TC = $24,000 + $8 * units
Sales Revenue = $0 + $12 * units

Note: An example breakeven graph is available on the book website.

14.   COST-VOLUME-PROFIT ANALYSIS: GRAPH

Same as assignment 13, but change total fixed cost from $24,000 to $10,000.
Note: The solution to this problem is at the end of the book.

15.   GRAPH COST BEHAVIOR PATTERNS

Graph each of the following cost behavior patterns over a relevant range from 0 to 10,000 units:

A. Variable expenses of $8 per unit
B. Mixed expenses made up of fixed costs of $10,000 and variable costs of $3 per unit
C. Fixed expenses of $35,000

16.   CONTRIBUTION MARGIN INCOME STATEMENT

Saville Row Shirtmakers' April income statement follows:

Saville Row Shirtmakers
Income Statement
April 20XX

Sales revenue		$640,000
Cost of goods sold		448,000
Gross margin		192,000
Operating expenses:		
Marketing expense	$72,000	
General and administrative expense	42,000	114,000
Operating income		$ 78,000

Saville Row's cost of goods sold is a variable expense. Marketing expense is 20% fixed and 80% variable. General and administrative expense is 60% fixed and 40% variable. Prepare Saville Row's contribution margin income statement for April. On the contribution margin income statement, include total sales revenue, total variable expenses, total contribution margin, total fixed expenses, and operating income. Calculate the expected increase in operating income to the nearest $1,000 if sales increase by $50,000.

Optional What-if Scenario:
What is the impact of changing the sales revenue from $640,000 to $740,000?

17.   DEPARTMENTAL INCOME STATEMENT

Portland Gear has two departments, Electronics and Industrial. The company's income statement for 20XX appears as follows:

Net sales............................	$350,000
Cost of goods sold..............	116,000
Gross margin	234,000
Operating expenses:...........	
Salaries expense	$ 75,000
Depreciation expense	15,000
Advertising expense	6,000
Other expenses	10,000
Total operating expenses..	106,000
Operating income...............	$128,000

Sales are Electronics, $136,000 and Industrial, $214,000. Cost of goods sold is distributed $42,000 to Electronics and $74,000 to Industrial. Salaries are traced directly to departments: Electronics, $33,000; Industrial, $42,000. Electronics accounts for 80% of advertising. Depreciation is allocated on the basis of square footage: Electronics has 20,000 square feet; Industrial has 40,000 square feet. Other expenses are allocated based on the number of employees. An equal number of employees work in each of the two departments.

A   Prepare departmental income statements that show revenues, expenses, and operating income for each of the company's two departments.

B.   In a departmental performance report, which are the most important expenses for evaluating Portland Gear's department managers? Give your reason.

Optional What-if Scenario:
What happens when sales revenue in Electronics is increased to $144,000 along with an increase of sales revenue in Industrial to $256,000? (All other items are unchanged.)

18.   FLEXIBLE BUDGET

Kandlestix Company, sells its main product, an elaborate candle, for $7.50 each. Its variable cost is $2 per candle. Fixed expenses are $200,000 per month for volumes up to 60,000 candles. Above 60,000 candles, monthly fixed expenses are $240,000. Prepare a monthly flexible budget for the product, showing sales, variable expenses, fixed expenses, and operating income or loss for volume levels of 40,000, 50,000, and 70,000 candles.

Optional What-if Scenario:
What is the impact of changing the sales price to $20 and the variable cost per unit to $15?

19.   GRAPH TOTAL COST LINE

Graph the flexible budget total cost line for the Kandlestix Company in assignment 18. Show total costs for volume levels of 0 (zero); 40,000; 50,000; 60,000; 60,001; and 70,000 candles.

20.   PRODUCT MIX ANALYSIS

Four Seasons Fashions sells both designer and moderately priced women's wear. Profits have fluctuated recently, and top management is deciding which product line to emphasize. Accountants have provided the following data:

	Per Item	
	Designer	Moderately Priced
Average sale price	$200	$80
Average variable expenses	70	24
Average contribution margin	$130	$56
Average fixed expenses (allocated)	20	10
Average gross margin	$110	$46

The Four Seasons store in Boca Raton, Florida, has 10,000 square feet of floor space. If it emphasizes moderately priced goods, 500 items can be displayed in the store. In contrast, if it emphasizes designer wear, only 200 designer items can be displayed for sale. These numbers are also the average monthly sales in units.

Prepare product mix analysis that identifies which product to emphasize (i.e., the product with the highest total contribution margin).

Optional What-if Scenario:
What happens when the unit contribution margin for a moderately priced item is changed from $56 to $46?

21.   MAKE OR BUY ANALYSIS

Skiptronics Industrial Controls manufactures an electronic control that it uses in its final product. The electronic control has the following manufacturing costs per unit:

Direct materials	$ 5.00
Direct labor	1.00
Variable overhead	1.50
Fixed overhead	4.00
Manufacturing product cost	$11.50

An outside supplier can sell Skiptronics the electronic control for $8 per unit. If Skiptronics buys the control from the outside supplier, the manufacturing facilities that will be idled cannot be used for any other purpose. Should Skiptronics make or buy the electronic controls? Explain the difference between correct analysis and incorrect analysis of this decision.

Optional What-if Scenario:
What is the impact of changing the purchase price from $8 to $6?

22.   BEST USE OF FACILITIES ANALYSIS

Assume that Skiptronics can make the electronic control unit (which it uses in its final product) for an incremental cost of $7.50 or purchase the unit from an outside supplier for $8.00. Skiptronics needs 90,000 electronic controls. By purchasing them from the outside supplier, Skiptronics can use its idle facilities to manufacture another product that will contribute $75,000 to operating income. Identify the *incremental* costs that Skiptronics will incur to acquire 90,000 electronic controls under three alternative plans: (a) make the controls; (b) buy the controls and leave the facilities idle; or (c) buy the controls and use facilities to manufacture another product. Which plan makes the best use of Skiptronic's facilities? Prepare a worksheet to support your answer.

Optional What-if Scenario:
What is the impact of changing the incremental cost of buying from $8 to $8.50?

23.   FLEXIBLE BUDGET

Broomstix Company sells its main product, a broom stick, for $8 each. Its variable cost is $2 per stick. Fixed expenses are $200,000 per month for volumes up to 60,000 sticks. Above 60,000 sticks, monthly fixed expenses are $240,000. Prepare a monthly flexible budget for the product, showing sales, variable expenses, fixed expenses, and operating income or loss for volume levels of 40,000, 50,000, and 70,000 boom sticks.

24.   FLEXIBLE BUDGET

Same as previous assignment, except the variable cost per unit is increased from $2 per broom stick to $3 per broom stick.

25.   FINANCIAL RATIOS

Use the following formulas to compute financial ratios for Junior's Computer Store for 20X2. The balance sheet and income statement for 20X2 and 20X1 are provided. Design the worksheet so that the financial statements are in the input area and the financial ratios are in the output area.

FINANCIAL RATIOS

Liquidity Ratios:

Current Ratio	=	(Cur. Assets)/(Cur. Liabilities)
Acid-Test Ratio	=	(Cur. Assets - Inven. - Prepaid Exp.)/(Cur. Liabilities)

Activity Ratios:

Receivables Turnover	=	(Net Credit Sales)/(Avg. A/R)
Inventory Turnover	=	(Cost of Goods Sold)/(Avg. Inventory)
Asset Turnover	=	(Net Sales)/(Avg. Assets)

Profitability Ratios:

Earnings Per Share	=	(Net Inc. - Pref. Div.)/(Com Shares Outstanding)
Price to Earnings (P/E)	=	(Market Price per Com. Share)/(EPS)
Dividend Payout	=	(Div. per Com. Share)/(EPS)
Sales Profit Margin	=	(Net Income)/(Net Sales)
Return on Assets	=	(Net Income + Int. Exp. - Tax Savings from Int. Exp.)/(Avg. Assets)
Return on Com Stk Equity	=	(Net Inc. - Pref. Div.)/(Avg. Com. Stk Equity)

Financial Stability Ratios:

Total Debt to Total Assets	=	(Total Liabilities)/(Total Assets)
Times Interest Earned	=	(Earnings before Int. and Taxes)/(Interest Charges)
Book Value Per Share	=	(Com. Stk Equity)/(Com. Shares Out.)
Cash Flow Per Share	=	(Net Income + Noncash Charges)/(Com. Shares Outstanding)

FINANCIAL STATEMENTS

Junior's Computer Store
Comparative Balance Sheets
12/31/X2 and 12/31/X1

	12/31/X2	12/31/X1
ASSETS:		
Cash	$1,200,000	$ 1,100,000
Accounts Receivable	780,000	550,000
Inventory	1,850,000	1,600,000
Fixed Assets (net)	8,200,000	7,200,000
Total Assets	$12,030,000	$10,450,000
LIABILITIES:		
Accounts Payable	$1,200,000	$900,000
Long-Term Debt	1,730,000	430,000
Total Liabilities	$2,930,000	$1,330,000
STOCKHOLDERS EQUITY:		
Preferred stock, $100 par, 12% cum	$1,800,000	$1,800,000
Common stock, $100 par	7,000,000	7,000,000
Retained Earnings	300,000	320,000
Total	$9,100,000	$9,120,000
Total Liabilities + Stockholders Equity	$12,030,000	$10,450,000
Market Price of Common Stock	$109	$107

Junior's Computer Store
Comparative Income Statements
FYE 12/31/X2 and 12/31/X1

	12/31/X2	12/31/X1
Sales	$4,000,000	$3,300,000
Cost of Goods Sold	2,200,000	1,650,000
Gross Profit	$1,800,000	$1,650,000

Operating Expenses:		
Depreciation	$738,000	$576,000
Advertising	45,000	38,000
Other	120,000	140,000
Total Operating Expense	$903,000	$754,000
Operating Income	$897,000	$896,000
Interest on Long-Term Debt	80,000	80,000
Income Before Taxes	$817,000	$816,000
Taxes	326,800	326,400
Net Income	$490,200	$489,600
Dividends Declared on Preferred Stock	$220,000	$220,000
Dividends on Common Stock	290,200	299,600
Net Income to Retained Earnings	($20,000)	($30,000)

NOTE: All sales are credit sales; the tax rate is 40%.

26.   FINANCIAL RATIOS

Same as previous assignment, but change the following 20X2 items:
    (a) Accounts Receivable: $780,000 to $1,780,000
    (b) Accounts Payable: $1,200,000 to $1,400,000
    (c) Retained Earnings: $300,000 to $1,100,000
    (d) Sales: $4,000,000 to $5,000,000

Note: The change in these financial statement items will affect other items.

27.   COMMON-SIZE BALANCE SHEETS

Using the comparative balance sheets in assignment 25, prepare common-size balance sheets. To prepare common-size balance sheets, divide all items by the "total assets" amount; thus, total assets each year (i.e., 20X2 and 20X1) will be shown as 100 percent.

28.   COMMON-SIZE BALANCE SHEETS

Using the revisions to the 20X2 balance sheet given in assignment 26, prepare common-size balance sheets for 20X2 and 20X1.

29.   HORIZONTAL ANALYSIS OF INCOME STATEMENTS

Prepare a horizontal analysis of the following comparative income statement of Dynasty International. Round percentage changes to the nearest one-tenth percent (3 decimal places):

Dynasty International
Comparative Income Statement
Years Ended December 31, 20X2 and 20X1

	20X2	20X1
Total revenue.............................	$410,000	$373,000
Expenses:		
Cost of goods sold..................	$202,000	$188,000
Selling and general expenses..	98,000	93,000
Interest expense......................	7,000	4,000
Income tax expense................	42,000	37,000
Total expenses........................	349,000	322,000
Net income..............................	$ 61,000	$ 51,000

Why did net income increase by a higher percentage than total revenues during 20X2?

30.   STATEMENT OF CASH FLOWS -- INVESTING ACTIVITIES

During fiscal year 20X1, The Home Spigot which operates over 400 home improvement centers throughout the United States, reported net income of $604 million and paid $162 million to acquire other businesses. Home Spigot paid $1,103 million to open new stores and sold property, plant, and equipment for $50 million. The company purchased long-term investments in stocks and bonds at a cost of $94 million and sold other long-term investments for $454 million. During the year, the company also cashed in other investments for $96 million.

Prepare the investing activities section of The Home Spigot's statement of cash flows. Based on The Home Spigot's investing activities, does it appear that the company is growing or shrinking? How can you tell?

Optional What-if Scenario:
What is the impact of changing the capital expenditures from $1,103 to $1,250 million?

31.   STATEMENT OF CASH FLOWS

The income statement and additional data of Boyce Computing Company follow:

Boyce Computing Company
Income Statement
Year Ended September 30, 20X2

Revenues:		
Sales revenue......................................		$237,000
Expenses:		
Cost of goods sold............................	103,000	
Salary expense....................................	45,000	
Depreciation expense..........................	29,000	
Rent expense......................................	11,000	
Interest expense..................................	2,000	
Income tax expense............................	9,000	199,000
Net income.......................................		$ 38,000

Additional data during fiscal year 20X2:

a.   Collections from customers were $7,000 more than sales.

b.   Payments to suppliers were $5,000 less than the sum of cost of goods sold plus rent expense.

c.   Payment to employees were $1,000 more than salary expense.

d.   Interest expense and income tax expense equal their cash amounts.

e.   Acquisition of equipment is $116,000. Of this amount, $101,000 was paid in cash, $15,000 by signing a long-term note payable. Boyce sold no equipment during fiscal year 20X2.

f.   Proceeds from sales of land, $14,000.

g.   Proceeds from issuance of common stock, $35,000.

h.   Payment of long-term note payable, $20,000.

i.   Payment of dividends, $10,000.

j.   Decrease in cash balance, $4,000.

A.   Prepare Boyce Computing Company's statement of cash flows and accompanying schedule of noncash investing and financing activities. Report operating activities by the **direct** method.

B.   Evaluate Boyce Computing Company's cash flows for the year. In your evaluation, mention all three categories of cash flows, and give the reason for your evaluation.

Optional What-if Scenario:

What is the impact of changing collections from customers from $244,000 to $275,000?

Background for Assignments 32 to 37: Foreign Currency Translation

When a multinational corporation based in the U.S. owns more than 50 percent of the voting stock of a foreign company, a parent-subsidiary relationship exists. The parent company is usually required to prepare consolidated financial statements. Before this can be done, the financial statements of the foreign subsidiary must be recast using U.S. generally accepted accounting principles (GAAP). Next, the foreign accounts must be remeasured (translated) from the foreign currency into U.S. dollars. To make the translation, the first step is to identify three currencies:

   (a)   Currency of books and records (CBR) -- the CBR is the currency in which the foreign financial statements are denominated;

   (b)   Functional currency (FC) -- the FC is the one in which the subsidiary generally buys, sells, borrows, repays, etc.; and

   (c)   Reporting currency (RC) -- the RC is the one in which the consolidated financial statements are denominated.

There are basically three approaches to currency translation: (1) temporal rate method, (2) current rate method, and (3) use of both methods. The following three rules are used to determine the method of translation:

   Rule 1:   If the FC is hyper-inflationary (i.e., 100% cumulative inflation within three years), then ignore the FC and remeasure the CBR into the RC using the temporal rate method.

   Rule 2:   If the CBR is different from the FC, then remeasure the CBR into the FC using the temporal rate method.

   Rule 3:   Translate from the FC into the RC using the current rate method.

You must apply the rules in sequence, stopping when the subsidiary's financial statements have been converted into the parent's reporting currency (RC). For example, when the functional currency (FC) is hyper-inflationary, then Rule 1 applies; that is, the financial statements which are denominated in the CBR are translated into the RC using the temporal rate method, and Rules 2 and 3 aren't used. A second example is as follows: If the CBR is British pounds, the FC is Dutch guilders (not hyper-inflationary), and the RC is U.S. dollars; then you skip Rule 1 and apply Rule 2, translating the CBR (pounds) into the FC (guilders) using the temporal rate method. Since the FC (guilders) is not the RC (dollars), you would then apply Rule 3 to translate the FC (guilders) into the RC (dollars) using the current rate method. A third example is as follows: When the CBR is the same as the FC, then you go directly to Rule 3.

Using the current rate method, all assets and liabilities are translated using the current rate (i.e., exchange rate on the balance sheet date). Owners' equity and dividends are translated at historical rates (exchange rate at the time the asset was acquired, liability incurred, or element of paid-in capital was issued or reacquired). Income statement items can be translated using the average exchange rate (the average of the exchange rate at the beginning of the accounting period and the current rate).

Under the temporal rate method, the objective is to measure each subsidiary transaction as though the transaction had been made by the parent. Monetary items (e.g. cash, receivables, inventories carried at market, payables, and long-term debt) are re-measured using the current exchange rate. Other items (e.g. prepaid expenses, inventories carried at cost, fixed assets, and stock) are re-measured using historical exchange rates.

Since different exchange rates are applied to different accounts, the resulting dollar-denominated trial balance will not likely balance. The debit or credit required to bring the dollar-denominated accounts into balance is the cumulative translation adjustment. The change in the cumulative translation adjustment during the current accounting period is the translation gain or loss. Under the current rate method, the translation gain or loss is accumulated on a separate line in the owner's equity section of the balance sheet and has no impact on the income statement. Under the temporal rate method, the translation gain or loss is shown on the income statement.

32.   FOREIGN CURRENCY TRANSLATION USING THE CURRENT RATE METHOD

First, read the above background information for this problem . Translate the following account balances from Dutch guilders to U.S. dollars using the current rate method.

Adjusted Trial Balance
In Dutch Guilders (DG)
December 31, Year 4

	Debit	Credit
Cash	20,000	
Accounts Receivable	35,000	
Inventory	105,000	
Equipment	60,000	
Accum. Dep.		20,000
Accounts Payable		35,000
Bonds Payable		50,000
Revenues		120,000

Adjusted Trial Balance - Continued

General Expenses	108,000	
Depreciation Expense	8,000	
Dividends	4,000	
Common Stock		62,000
Paid-in Capital in Excess of Par		44,000
Retained Earnings		9,000
Total	340,000	340,000

Exchange Rates:

	1 DG = $___
Current Exchange Rate	0.520
Average Exchange Rate	0.490
At July 31, Year 4	0.505
At June 30, Year 1	0.470

Other: All common stock was issued on June 30, Year 1 (i.e., 6/30/Y1).
          Dividends were declared and paid on July 31, Year 4.
          Translated Retained Earnings at 12/31/Y4 was: $5,500.

33.   FOREIGN CURRENCY TRANSLATION USING THE CURRENT RATE METHOD

Same as previous assignment, except the exchange rates are as follows:

Current Exchange Rate	1.200
Average Exchange Rate	1.250
At July 31, Year 4	1.300
At June 30, Year 1	1.000

Note: The solution to this problem is at the end of the book.

34.   FOREIGN CURRENCY TRANSLATION USING THE CURRENT RATE METHOD

Use the following information to translate from British pounds to U.S. dollars using the current rate method. Background information starts on page 69.

Adjusted Trial Balance
In British Pounds
December 31, Year 8

	Debit	Credit
Cash	72,000	
Accounts Receivable	60,000	
Inventory	136,000	
Fixed Assets	130,000	
Accum. Dep.		76,000
Accounts Payable		50,000
Bonds Payable		90,000
Revenues		172,000
General Expenses	158,000	
Depreciation Expense	10,000	
Dividends	4,000	
Common Stock		58,000
Paid-in Capital in Excess of Par		98,000
Retained Earnings		26,000
Total	570,000	570,000

Exchange Rates:

	1 BP = $___
Current Exchange Rate	2.100
Average Exchange Rate	2.000
At July 31, Year 8	2.050
At June 30, Year 1	1.500

Other: All common stock was issued on June 30, Year 1 (i.e., 6/30/Y1).
        Dividends were declared and paid on July 31, Year 8.
        Translated Retained Earnings at 12/31/Y8 was $22,600.

35. FOREIGN CURRENCY TRANSLATION USING THE CURRENT RATE METHOD

Same as previous assignment, except use the following exchange rates:

Current Exchange Rate	3.100
Average Exchange Rate	2.900
At July 31, Year 8	2.950
At June 30, Year 1	4.000

36. FOREIGN CURRENCY TRANSLATION USING THE TEMPORAL RATE METHOD

Use the temporal rate method to remeasure from the currency of books and records (i.e., British pounds) to the functional currency (i.e., U.S. dollars). Background information starts on page 69.

Adjusted Trial Balance
In British Pounds
December 31, Year 4

	Debit	Credit
Cash	52,000	
Accounts Receivable	60,000	
Inventory		
(10-31-Y3)	40,000	
(7-31-Y4)	160,000	
Fixed Assets		
(6-30-Y1)	13,000	
(12-31-Y1)	65,000	
(7-31-Y2)	52,000	
Accum. Dep.		
(6-30-Y1)		8,000
(12-31-Y1)		40,000
(7-31-Y2)		32,000
Accounts Payable		43,000
Bonds Payable		160,000
Revenues		214,000

Adjusted Trial Balance - Continued

General Expenses	189,000	
Depreciation Expense		
(6-30-Y1)	1,500	
(12-31-Y1)	7,500	
(7-31-Y2)	6,000	
Dividends (7-31-Y4)	10,000	
Common Stock		
(6-30-Y1)		48,000
(1-31-Y2)		32,000
Paid-in Capital in Excess of Par		
(6-30-Y1)		30,000
(1-31-Y2)		20,000
Retained Earnings		29,000
Total	656,000	656,000

Exchange Rates	1 BP = $____
Current Exchange Rate	0.600
Average Exchange Rate	0.610
At July 31, Year 4	0.606
At October 31, Year 3	0.591
At July 31, Year 2	0.585
At January 31, Year 2	0.586
At December 31, Year 1	0.590
At June 30, Year 1	0.580

Other:

    Regarding common stock, 60% was issued 6/30/Y1; 40% on 1/31/Y2.

    Regarding inventory, 20% was acquired 10/31/Y3; 80% on 7/31/Y4.

    Dividends were declared and paid on 7/31/Y4.

    Regarding fixed assets, 10% were acquired 6/30/Y1; 50% on 12/31/Y1; and 40% on 7/31/Y2.

    Revenues and expenses were accrued evenly throughout the year.

    Translated retained earnings at 12/31/Y4 was $16,400

37. FOREIGN CURRENCY TRANSLATION USING THE TEMPORAL RATE METHOD

Same as previous assignment, except use the following exchange rates:

	1 BP = $___
Current Exchange Rate	2.000
Average Exchange Rate	2.400
At July 31, Year 4	2.300
At October 31, Year 3	2.150
At July 31, Year 2	2.200
At January 31, Year 2	2.180
At December 31, Year 1	2.250
At June 30, Year 1	2.100

Background for Assignments 38 to 42: Comparative Advantage

Productivity provides an economic basis for trade. During the early 1800s, David Ricardo and other economists provided an explanation for trade based on different levels of productivity among nations in different industries. This can be illustrated as follows. First, assume that there is only one factor of production, labor. Next, assume that a worker in the country of Bigred can produce either 8 bales of cotton or 4 crates of apples, and that a worker in the country of Bigblue can produce either 1 bale of cotton or 1 crate of apples. Table A shows production in Bigred and Bigblue.

Table A Cotton and Apples as Produced by Bigred and Bigblue		
	Bigred Worker	Bigblue Worker
Cotton	8 bales	1 bale
Apples	4 crates	1 crate

Opportunity costs of production are shown in Table B.

Table B
Opportunity Costs of Production in Bigred and Bigblue

Bigred: 8 bales of cotton cost 4 crates of apples, so
               1 bale of cotton costs 1/2 crate of apples.
               4 crates of apples cost 8 bales of cotton, so
               1 crate of apples costs 2 bales of cotton.
Bigblue: 1 bale of cotton costs 1 crate of apples.
               1 crate of apples costs 1 bale of cotton.

Table A shows that a worker in Bigred is more productive in both cotton and apples than a worker in Bigblue. The Bigred worker has an "absolute advantage" in productivity in both industries. When industries are compared, the Bigred worker is found to be relatively more productive in the cotton industry (8 to 1) than in the apple industry (4 to 1) in relation to the Bigblue worker. Thus, the Bigred worker has a "comparative advantage" in the cotton industry. Thus, Bigred's absolute advantage in cotton is proportionately greater than its absolute advantage in apples.

A lower skilled and lower productive nation will have a comparative advantage in something because there will be some industry in which it is least disadvantaged. If Bigred is better at producing apples than Bigblue, why won't Bigred produce its own apples? The answer is that Bigred determines it more advantageous to produce what it does best, cotton, and trading this cotton for apples. Table C, which is derived from Table B, shows what prices would have to be in effect for trade to be beneficial.

Table C
Prices at Which Trade Would Occur

Bigred: If 1 bale of cotton sells for more than 1/2 crate of apples, Bigred gains by
                   selling cotton.
               If 1 crate of apples sells for less than 2 bales of cotton, Bigred gains by
                   buying apples.
Bigblue: If 1 bale of cotton sells for less than 1 crate of apples, Bigblue gains by
                   buying cotton.
               If 1 crate of apples sells for more than 1 bale of cotton, Bigblue gains by
                   selling apples.
Thus: If the price of apples on the world markets is between 1 bale of cotton and
                   2 bales of cotton, and if the price of apples is between 1/2 crate of
                   apples and 1 crate of apples, trade is mutually advantageous.

Table D shows the change in world output if firms in each nation reallocate workers to the industry in which the nation has a comparative advantage. The Bigred cotton industry hires a worker away from the apple industry, and the Bigblue apple industry hires five workers away from the cotton industry. Consequently, the world output of cotton increases by 3 bales, and the world output of apples increases by 1 crate.

Table D
Increase in World Production Based on Transfers of
One Worker in Bigred and Five Workers in Bigblue

	One Bigred Worker	Five Bigblue Workers	World Output
Cotton (bales)	+1	-5	+3
Apples (crates)	-1	+5	+1

Assume that the Bigred firm exports 4 bales of cotton to Bigblue, and that the price of a bale of cotton is 0.7 crates of apples. The trade yields Bigred 2.8 crates of apples. Before international trade, the Bigred firm could have obtained only 2 crates of apples for its 4 bales of cotton. Before international trade, the Bigblue could have obtained only 2.8 bales of cotton for its 2.8 crates of apples, but now gets 4 bales of cotton for its 2.8 crates. The price determines which country receives the greatest benefit. For example, if 1 bale of cotton equals to 0.8 crates of apples, Bigred would have benefitted more from the trade than where the price was 0.7 crates. However, as long at the price falls within the range shown in Table C, both countries gain from specialization and trade. If the costs of production of cotton and apples remained constant, eventually all cotton would be produced in Bigred and all apples in Bigblue. However, increasing costs will probably occur at some point; the cost of producing cotton in Bigred will increase, and the cost of producing apples in Bigblue will increase. At this point, trade is curtailed. Consequently, it is rarely the case that one country produces all of one product.

Effects of an Import Quota

Given the above presentation of comparative advantage, you can understand why the great majority of economists strongly support free trade and oppose the use of tariffs and quotas that impede the free exchange of goods and services. However, there are political motivations that advocate protection of domestic industry. The political motivations for advocating protectionism generally are not supported by sound economic analysis.

38.   ECONOMIC IMPACT OF AN IMPORT QUOTA

First, read the background information for this problem starting on page 75.
Use the following equation to prepare a domestic demand curve:
P(QD) = 100 - 10 * Q

Use the following equations to prepare a domestic supply and a world supply curve:
P(QS-d) = 0 + 10 * Q
P(QS-w) = 20 + 0*Q

The demand curve represents the home country's demand for a homogeneous good (e.g. corn, iron, rubber, etc.). The domestic supply curve is a typical upward-sloping curve. The world market price is $20; thus, persons may import as much as they want at a constant price of $20. In other words, the world supply curve is perfectly elastic at a price of $20. Assume that an import quota of 4 units is established.

Prepare the following:
A.   Table of Q (from 0 to 10, in increments of 1), P(QD), P(QS-domestic), and P(QS-world).
B.   Graph the domestic demand curve (P(QD), domestic supply curve (P(QS-d), world supply curve (P(QS-w), and a vertical line at the quantity of 4 to illustrate the effect of the quota.
C.   What is equilibrium price and quantity before and after the quota?
D.   Who are the winners and losers from the quota?

39.   ECONOMIC IMPACT OF AN IMPORT QUOTA

Same as previous assignment, except for the following changes:
1.   The demand equation is as follows: P(QD) = 120 - 10*Q
2.   The world market price is $30.
3.   The domestic supply and world supply equations are as follows:
P(QS-d) = 20 + 10*Q
P(QS-w) = 30 + 0*Q
4.   The quota is set at 3 units.

Note: The solution to this problem is at the end of the book.

40.   ECONOMIC IMPACT OF A TARIFF

Read the background information for this assignment starting on page 75.
Use the following information and analyze the impact of a tariff. Use the following equation
to prepare a domestic demand curve:

   $P(QD) = 120 - 1*Q$

Use the following equations to prepare a supply curve before and after the tariff is
implemented. The tariff is set at $20.

   $P(QS) = 20 + 1*Q$
   $P(QS)+T = (20 + 1*Q) + T$

Prepare the following:
A.   Table of Q (from 0 to 100, in increments of 10), P(QD), P(QS), and P(QS)+T.
B.   Graph of the demand curve, P(QD); supply curve before tariff, P(QS); and supply
       curve after tariff, P(QS)+T.
C.   What is equilibrium price and quantity before and after the tariff?
D.   What is the protective effect and revenue effect of the tariff?

41.   ECONOMIC IMPACT OF A TARIFF

Same as assignment 40, except the tariff is set at $40 rather than $20.

42.   ECONOMIC IMPACT OF A TARIFF

Same as assignment 40, except the tariff is set at $60 rather than $20.

Case Problem

The following case problem assumes that you have been hired as a controller for a small retail florist firm. Your immediate task is described in the "welcome" letter sent to you from the president of the company, shown below.

Maroon Mums, Inc.
"Defining Elegance in School Spirit"

Hello: November 3, 20X1

I would like to welcome you to Maroon Mums, Inc. (MMI) as our new Controller. Although, I wish I could be in town to welcome you to the company personally, I am excited that I may be able to secure some additional capital from some investors in New York. I have provided a brief company history for your review and also left copies of the prior year financials on your desk. I am sure you will be busy this week getting settled in, but as you know from your experience as a controller, the work never stops. I already have your first project ready.

The investors up here (Gold & Cashe, LP) would like to see some budgeted numbers for the upcoming year. I have provided the following information to help you get started. First, you will find a company information and history document. This is mostly to help familiarize you with Maroon Mums, Inc. It has important information including our pricing, information from our market research, and other operations information that you will need to know. In addition, I have left a copy of the prior year budget worksheets which are contained in an Excel workbook file named PYMAROON.XLS. Based on that, the company information, and the attached request list, I think you will be able to pull together the budget information that Gold & Cashe has requested.

Keep in mind that Gold & Cashe have requested different schedules for different periods of the year. The prior year example provides information for the second quarter. You will need to use the numbers given on the request list for the worksheets that you are preparing. I thank you for your hard work in advance. I know this will not be easy to do in your first week at the company, but this financing will be very beneficial to our firm.

As a final note, make sure you input prices, etc. at the top of the page and use these in the formulas. That way if we need to make some changes (say we want to see the effect of changing some of the prices), we only have to change the number at the top and the formulas will update. Also, I had the accounting manager prepare the budget templates for you and highlight the areas where you will need to input values and formulas.

Enjoy your first week at the company!

Best Wishes,

Griff
Griffin Diaz, C.P.A
President & CEO

History

Maroon Mums, Inc. (MMI) was founded five years ago. The idea was created when Meg Alexander was able to genetically create various flower species in a deep maroon color. Originally, Meg focused mostly on using this science to color mums and pass them out at football games for her favorite college team Bell University. The flowers became extremely popular at the games and soon "die-hard" fans were requesting different flower arrangements of the maroon flowers for Valentines Day, Mothers Day, and to use at weddings. Meg realized she had found a gold mine, but had no business savvy and realized she needed help.

Meg contacted her friend Griffin Diaz, an MBA graduate of Bell University and he accepted the position of CEO in 1998 and helped Meg incorporate in 1999. Since taking the job at MMI, Griffin has expanded the company extensively. Meg has remained Chief Operations Officer and Research Director, but Griffin has managed all other aspects of the business. For the first few years, Griffin maintained the books of the company (he is a CPA and previously worked for the well known accounting firm, Greene & Byrd, LLP). He hired an accounting manager about 2 years ago to take care of the day-to-day aspects of the accounting, but Griffin remained the person in charge of the budget and major accounting decisions including policies and disclosures. As the business continues to expand into new markets (Meg now has the ability to create blue and gold flowers), Griffin needs to shift his attention toward a possible IPO and to developing new markets. In September and October of 20X1, Griffin set out to hire a controller (you) to take over his responsibilities in the accounting and finance areas.

Demand and Seasonality

MMI has a very seasonal business. The arrangements sell all year long for events such as birthdays and anniversaries, as fans of the team like the school colors in the arrangements. There are very busy times of the year however. February is busy due to Valentine's Day. This is typically a very high sales month for floral and greetings card retailers. Mother's Day is another popular holiday involving flower arrangements. May also kicks off the summer and many people who attend the University, like the Maroon flowers in their wedding ceremonies which typically occur after school is out. This higher sales season goes through August. September begins football games and the original "Maroon Mums" sell like crazy as everyone comes out to support the Bell U football team. This usually ends at the end of November with the last football game. December and January are slow months for MMI. MMI is usually is usually in a break-even or loss position during the slow months, but more than makes up for this during the high demand months.

Pricing

Due to the large variations in demand, higher prices are charged in the summer for weddings and during the fall for football season. The price list by month is as follows for each arrangement:

January/March/April/December	$25
February	$35
May	$30
June/July/August	$50
September/October/November	$40

Expected Sales Growth

The company has invested in a significant amount of market research. This research has told them that with the right marketing and proper work force, they can increase sales from the prior year 5% in the slow months (months where only $25 is charged per arrangement) and 15% on average in the busy months. MMI prepared the budget on these assumptions in the prior year and found that this was a good benchmark for actual sales in units. The research done estimates that the market will not become saturated until at least 20x4, so Griffin feels that this should be used again to set budgetary goals.

Materials, Labor & Production

The company uses very little materials. The main type of material used is a special type of florist ribbon. Each arrangement uses about 36 inches of ribbon. The ribbon is purchased in large quantities and costs the company $.19 per inch of ribbon. Each of the arrangements must be done by hand. This requires about 45 minutes per arrangement. Flower arrangers will be paid $5.75/hour in 20x2; a small increase from 20x1.

The company generally tries to keep at least 5% of the budgeted next month's production in inventory. Because of the short lifetime of the flowers they cannot keep more than 5% in production inventory. Generally, this is just enough to cover the first one to two days of the next month. The materials inventory (ribbon) is maintained at 50% of the next months expected production. This is feasible because the ribbon is non-perishable and takes very little storage area.

Variable Overhead is $4.30/hour. Other overhead expenses include property tax of $4,250/month and equipment depreciation of $5,655/month (this is mostly for office equipment and furniture, computers, buildings, and delivery vans), and indirect labor of $56,750. These are the 2002 estimates and are different from prior year.

Cash Flows and Collections

The company generally is paid for about 20% of sales in cash. These customers are rewarded with a 1% discount. The remaining 80% of sales are paid on credit. Those customers that pay within the month are also offered the 1% discount. This accounts for about 60% of the credit sales. The remaining amount is collected in the following month after sale, but history has shown that 2% of the credit sales are not collectable.

CASE REQUIREMENTS

Below, you are given eight specific worksheets to create. You should first create an Excel workbook (name it MAROON20X2.XLS) and then create all the worksheets within that workbook. You should use the same format as shown in the prior year workpapers, which are provided on the following pages. The file containing the prior year workpapers (PYMAROON.XLS) and the file containing worksheets that you are to complete (MAROON20X2.XLS) are available on this book's website. These files will save you some time in entering data, but of course, you can complete the case by creating the workbook and related worksheets, starting from a blank Excel worksheet.

1. Prepare a Sales Forecast in units of Mum Arrangements per month for the whole year. Our seasonal needs are discussed in the company background along with our budgeting forecast policy. Create (or retrieve from this book's website) an Excel workbook file and title it MAROON20X2.XLS. Prepare the Sales Forecast and save it to a worksheet labeled "Forecast" in the MAROON20X2.XLS excel workbook file.

2. Prepare a Sales Budget for gross sales for the Second Quarter of 20x2. Use the company price list to estimate the Sales Budget. Gold & Cashe would like us to assume that we sell 5,500; 16,250; and 19,000 Mum Arrangements in April, May and June, respectively. Don't worry if this does not equal your estimate in the previous request. They are going to take this information and do some modeling with it, so just go with their assumptions. Prepare the Sales Budget on a worksheet labeled "Sales" in the MAROON20X2.XLS excel workbook file.

3. Prepare a Budgeted Net Sales schedule for the third quarter. One of our best quarters is the third quarter when we go from covering the wedding bouquet demand straight into football season. I told the Gold & Cashe representatives that our sales are great, but they want to see estimates after we take out bad debts and discounts. Use estimated sales of $916,400; $900,900; and $1,369,420 for July, August, and September, respectively. Prepare the Budgeted Net Sales on a worksheet titled "NetSales" in the MAROON20X2.XLS excel workbook file.

4.   Prepare a cash collections budget for the fourth quarter of 20x2. The investors are curious about collections in the last quarter especially since December and January are slow months for MMI. Even though you may have other estimates based on your previous budgeting in earlier schedules, they have sales targets that they would like us to reach. Prepare this schedule similar to the one I did last year with one section showing the collections from cash sales and the other showing collections on credit sales. Then add the columns to get total monthly cash collections. Also, mark with an asterisk (*) the amount of accounts receivables for each month of the quarter similar to how it was done in the prior year file. Assume that sales are $1,570,350; $1,748,700; and $108,675 for October, November and December of 20x2 respectively. September sales should be assumed to be the same as in item number 3 above. When you are done budgeting the cash collections save it to a worksheet called "Collections" in the MAROON20X2.XLS excel workbook file.

5.   Prepare a schedule for budgeted production. Gold & Cashe are especially interested in budgeted production for the second quarter of 20x2. You should assume that we will sell the same number of Mum Arrangements in the second quarter as we assumed for item number 2. You should also assume that March finished goods inventory is 300 units and July forecasted sales are 19,328 units. Prepare the Production Budget on a worksheet labeled "Production" in the MAROON20X2.XLS excel workbook file.

6.   Prepare the budget for direct materials purchases for the second quarter. You should assume that production is 6,000; 16,400; and 19,020 for April, May and June 20x2, respectively. You should review our company policies on materials inventory and for materials costs. July sales units should be estimated to be 19,328 (the same assumption as in item number 5). March ending inventory should be assumed to be 92,600 inches of ribbon. When the Direct Materials Purchases Budget has been prepared, save the worksheet as "Materials" in the MAROON20X2.XLS excel workbook file.

7.   Provide an estimate of Budgeted Direct Labor costs. All the information needed for the calculation should be in the company background information. Assume production units are 6,000; 16,400; and 19,020 for April, May and June, (the same as you did in item number 6). Prepare this Direct Labor Budget for the second quarter only and save it in a worksheet called "Labor" in the MAROON20X2.XLS excel workbook file.

8.   Prepare a Budgeted Overhead Schedule. Assume that the following are the labor hours needed for April, May and June, respectively: 6,125; 13,220; 14,375. Most of the information you will require for this schedule is in the company background

information. Prepare the Factory Overhead Budget for the second quarter of 20X2 and save it to a worksheet called "Overhead" in the MAROON20X2.XLS excel workbook file.

The prior year workpapers are provided as follows.

FILE IDENTIFICATION AREA:

NAME:	LUCA PACIOLI
DATE CREATED:	JAN. 1, 20X1
FILENAME:	PYMAROON.XLS
WORKSHEET:	FILES

   LISTING OF SPREADSHEETS IN PYMAROON.XLS WORKBOOK FILE

INPUT/OUTPUT AREA:

PRIOR YEAR WORKING PAPERS
   SECOND QUARTER, 20X1

SPREADSHEET NAME	DESCRIPTION
--------------------------------	---------------------------------------
FORECAST	SALES FORECAST
SALES	SALES BUDGET
NETSALES	NET SALES WORKSHEET
COLLECTIONS	CASH COLLECTIONS BUDGET
PRODUCTION	PRODUCTION BUDGET
MATERIALS	DIRECT MATERIALS PURCHASES BUDGET
LABOR	DIRECT LABOR BUDGET
OVERHEAD	FACTORY OVERHEAD BUDGET

FILE IDENTIFICATION AREA:

NAME: LUCA PACIOLI
DATE CREATED: JAN.1, 20X1
FILENAME: PYMAROON.XLS
WORKSHEET: FORECAST
CLIENT: MAROON MUMS INC.
                   PRIOR YEAR WORKING PAPERS - UNIT SALES FORECAST

INPUT AREA:

Regular Growth	5%
High Growth	15%

OUTPUT AREA:

UNIT SALES FORECAST

MONTH	20X0 UNIT SALES (actual)	20X1 UNIT SALES (budgeted)
QUARTER 1		
JANUARY	4,750	4,988
FEBRUARY	13,045	15,002
MARCH	5,905	6,200
QUARTER 2:		
APRIL	4,667	4,900
MAY	14,085	16,198
JUNE	15,215	17,497
QUARTER 3:		
JULY	13,740	15,801
AUGUST	13,565	15,600
SEPTEMBER	26,000	29,900
QUARTER 4:		
OCTOBER	23,950	27,543
NOVEMBER	26,200	30,130
DECEMBER	4,000	4,200

FILE IDENTIFICATION AREA:

NAME:	LUCA PACIOLI
DATE CREATED:	JAN. 1, 20X1
FILENAME:	PYMAROON.XLS
WORKSHEET:	SALES
CLIENT:	MAROON MUMS INC.
	PRIOR YEAR WORKING PAPERS - SALES BUDGET

INPUT AREA:

UNIT SALES FROM SALES FORECAST

SALES PRICE / REGULAR		$25.00
SALES PRICE / FEBRUARY		$35.00
SALES PRICE / MAY		$30.00
SALES PRICE / SUMMER		$50.00
SALES PRICE / FOOTBALL		$40.00
CASH SALES	20%	
CREDIT SALES	80%	

OUTPUT AREA:

SALES BUDGET
SECOND QUARTER, 20X1

	APRIL	MAY	JUNE
UNIT SALES FORECAST	4,900	16,198	17,497
SALES PRICE PER UNIT	$25	$30	$50
TOTAL SALES	$122,500	$485,940	$874,850
CASH SALES	$24,500	$97,188	$174,970
CREDIT SALES	98,000	388,752	699,880
TOTAL SALES	$122,500	$485,940	$874,850

FILE IDENTIFICATION AREA:

NAME:	LUCA PACIOLI
DATE CREATED:	JAN. 1, 20X1
FILENAME:	PYMAROON.XLS
WORKSHEET:	NETSALES
CLIENT:	MAROON MUMS INC.
	PRIOR YEAR WORKING PAPERS - BUDGETED NET SALES

INPUT AREA:

SALES AND SALES INFORMATION FROM SALES BUDGET:

CASH SALES	20%
CREDIT SALES	80%

SALES INFORMATION FROM CASH COLLECTION BUDGET:

ACCOUNTS RECEIVABLE COLLECTION EXPERIENCE IS	60%
COLLECTED IN MONTH OF SALE AND SUBJECT TO DISCOUNT OF	1%
COLLECTED IN THE NEXT MONTH (NO DISCOUNT)	38%
ESTIMATED UNCOLLECTIBLE	2%
ALL CASH SALES RECEIVE A DISCOUNT OF	1%

OUTPUT AREA:

BUDGETED NET SALES
SECOND QUARTER, 20X1

	APRIL	MAY	JUNE
SALES	$122,500	$485,940	$874,850
LESS:			
DISCOUNTS	833	3,304	5,949
BAD DEBTS	1,960	7,775	13,998
NET SALES	$119,707	$474,861	$854,903

FILE IDENTIFICATION AREA:

NAME:	LUCA PACIOLI
DATE CREATED:	JAN. 1, 20X1
FILENAME:	PYMAROON.XLS
WORKSHEET:	COLLECTIONS
CLIENT:	MAROON MUMS INC.
	PRIOR YEAR WORKING PAPERS - CASH COLLECTIONS BUDGET

INPUT AREA:

	SALES
MARCH	$150,000
APRIL	$122,500
MAY	$485,940
JUNE	$874,850
CREDIT SALES FROM SALES BUDGET	80%
CASH SALES FROM SALES BUDGET	20%
ACCOUNTS RECEIVABLE COLLECTION EXPERIENCE IS	60%
COLLECTED IN MONTH OF SALE AND SUBJECT TO DISCOUNT OF	1%
COLLECTED IN THE NEXT MONTH (NO DISCOUNT)	38%
ESTIMATED UNCOLLECTIBLE	2%
ALL CASH SALES RECEIVE A DISCOUNT OF	1%

OUTPUT AREA:

CASH COLLECTIONS BUDGET
SECOND QUARTER, 20X1

MONTH	CREDIT SALES	APRIL	MAY	JUNE
MARCH	$120,000	$45,600		
APRIL	$98,000	58,212	$37,240 *	
MAY	$388,752		230,919	$147,726 *
JUNE	$699,880			415,729
COLLECTIONS FROM				
CREDIT SALES		$103,812	$268,159	$563,454

MONTH	CREDIT SALES			
APRIL	24,500	24,255		
MAY	97,188		96,216	
JUNE	174,970			173,220
TOTAL CASH				
COLLECTIONS		$128,067	$364,375	$736,675

* Month end accounts receivable net of estimated uncollectibles, for April-June, respectively.

FILE IDENTIFICATION AREA:

NAME:	LUCA PACIOLI
DATE CREATED:	JAN. 1, 20X1
FILENAME:	PYMAROON.XLS
WORKSHEET:	PRODUCTION
CLIENT:	MAROON MUMS INC.
	PRIOR YEAR WORKING PAPERS -
	PRODUCTION BUDGET

INPUT AREA:

UNIT SALES FROM SALES FORECAST

DESIRED ENDING INVENTORY IS   5%
OF THE NEXT MONTH'S FORECASTED
UNIT SALES. JULY FORECASED SALES ARE   15,801 UNITS

MARCH FINISHED GOODS ENDING INVENTORY   245 units

OUTPUT AREA:

PRODUCTION BUDGET
SECOND QUARTER, 2002

	APRIL	MAY	JUNE
UNIT SALES FORECAST			
ADD:	4,900	16,198	17,497
DESIRED FINISHED GOODS ENDING INV.			
	810	875	790
TOTAL NEEDED			
	5,710	17,073	18,287
LESS:			
FINISHED GOODS BEGINNING INVENTORY			
	245	810	875
REQUIRED PRODUCTION			
	5,465	16,263	17,412

FILE IDENTIFICATION AREA:

NAME:	LUCA PACIOLI
DATE CREATED:	JAN. 1, 20X1
FILENAME:	PYMAROON.XLS
WORKSHEET:	MATERIALS
CLIENT:	MAROON MUMS, INC.
	PRIOR YEAR WORKING PAPERS -
	DIRECT MATERIALS PURCHASES BUDGET

INPUT AREA:

REQUIRED PRODUCTION FROM THE PRODUCTION BUDGET

RIBBON-INCES PER FINISHED UNIT (ALL MONTHS)	36	INCHES
COST PER RIBBON INCH (ALL MONTHS)	$0.19	
THE DESIRED ENDING INVENTORY OF DM IS	50%	
OF THE NEXT MONTH'S FORECASTED NEEDS.		
JULY FORECASTED SALES ARE	15,801	UNITS
MARCH DIRECT MATERIALS ENDING INVENTORY	98,375	INCHES

OUTPUT AREA:

DIRECT MATERIALS PURCHASES BUDGET
SECOND QUARTER, 20X1

	APRIL	MAY	JUNE
REQUIRED PRODUCTION	5,465	16,263	17,412
RIBBON INCHES PER FINISHED UNIT	36	36	36
DIRECT MATERIALS USED IN PRODUCTION	196,740	585,468	626,832
ADD:			
DESIRED DIRECT MATERIALS ENDING INVENTORY	292,734	313,416	284,418
TOTAL NEEDED	489,474	898,884	911,250
LESS:			
DIRECT MATERIALS BEGINNING INVENTORY	98,375	292,734	313,416
REQUIRED RIBBON-INCHES PURCHASES	391,099	606,150	597,834
COST PER RIBBON-INCH	$0.19	$0.19	$0.19
COST OF REQUIRED PURCHASES	$74,309	$115,169	$113,588

FILE IDENTIFICATION AREA:

NAME: LUCA PACIOLI
DATE CREATED: JAN. 1, 20X1
FILENAME: PYMAROON.XLS
WORKSHEET: LABOR
CLIENT: .   MAROON MUMS INC
                               PRIOR YEAR WORKING PAPERS - DIRECT LABOR BUDGET

INPUT AREA:

REQUIRED PRODUCTION FROM PRODUCTION BUDGET
DIRECT LABOR HOURS PER UNIT   0.75 hours
COST PER DIRECT LABOR HOUR $5.50

OUTPUT AREA:

DIRECT LABOR BUDGET
SECOND QUARTER, 20X1

	APRIL	MAY	JUNE
REQUIRED PRODUCTION	5,465	16,263	17,412
DIRECT LABOR HOURS / UNIT	0.75	0.75	0.75
TOTAL HOURS NEEDED	4,099	12,197	13,059
COST PER HOUR	$5.50	$5.50	$5.50
TOTAL DIRECT LABOR COST	$22,543	$67,085	$71,825

FILE IDENTIFICATION AREA:

NAME:	LUCA PACIOLI
DATE CREATED:	JAN. 1, 20X1
FILENAME:	PYMAROON.XLS
WORKSHEET:	OVERHEAD
CLIENT:	MAROON MUMS INC
	PRIOR YEAR WORKING PAPERS -
	FACTORY OVERHEAD BUDGET

INPUT AREA:

DIRECT LABOR HOURS NEEDED FROM DIRECT LABOR BUDGET	
VARIABLE OVERHEAD RATE PER DIRECT LABOR HOUR	$4.15
INDIRECT LABOR	$53,200
PROPERTY TAX	$4,175
EQUIPMENT DEPRECIATION	$4,980

OUTPUT AREA:

FACTORY OVERHEAD BUDGET
SECOND QUARTER, 20X1

	APRIL	MAY	JUNE
TOTAL DIRECT LABOR HOURS NEEDED	4,099	12,197	13,059
VARIABLE OVERHEAD RATE	$4.15	$4.15	$4.15
TOTAL VARIABLE OVERHEAD	$17,011	$50,618	$54,195
FIXED OVERHEAD:			
INDIRECT LABOR	53,200	53,200	53,200
PROPERTY TAX	4,175	4,175	4,175
TOTAL OVERHEAD REQUIRING CASH	$74,386	$107,993	$111,570
DEPRECIATION OF EQUIPMENT	4,980	4,980	4,980
TOTAL OVERHEAD	$79,366	$112,973	$116,550

SOLUTIONS

to

Selected Assignments

3.   COST-VOLUME PROFIT ANALYSIS

FILE IDENTIFICATION AREA:
Name:
Date Created:
Filename: A03.xls

INPUT AREA:

Sales Price Per Item	=	$20.00
Variable Cost Per Item	=	16.00
Total Fixed Cost	=	$24,000

OUTPUT AREA:

Sales Price	$20.00
Variable Cost	16.00
Contribution Margin	$4.00
Fixed Cost	$24,000
Breakeven Point in Units	6,000
Breakeven Point in Dollars	$120,000

7. COMPUTE EQUIVALENT UNITS: WEIGHTED AVERAGE

FILE IDENTIFICATION AREA:

Name:

Date Created:

Filename:

INPUT AREA: Units transferred in during May   80,000

OUTPUT AREA:

Harman's Hardwood Flooring
Finishing Department
Equivalent Units (Weighted Average)

	Flow of Physical Units	Equivalent Units		
Flow of production		Transferred In	Direct Materials	Conversion Costs
Units to account for:				
Beginning work in process, April 30	6,000			
Transferred in during May	80,000			
Total physical units to account for	86,000			
Units accounted for:				
Completed and transferred out during May:	81,000	81,000	81,000	81,000
Ending work in process, May 31	5,000	5,000	3,500 *	3,000 *
Total physical units accounted for	86,000			
Equivalent units		86,000	84,500	84,000

*Direct materials:	5000 units * 0.7 =	3500
Conversion costs:	5000 units * 0.6 =	3000

14.   COST-VOLUME-PROFIT ANALYSIS: GRAPH

FILE IDENTIFICATION AREA:
Name:

INPUT AREA:	Sales Price Per Item	=	$12.00
	Variable Cost Per Item	=	8.00
	Total Fixed Cost	=	$10,000
OUTPUT AREA:	Sales Price		$12.00
	Variable Cost		8.00
	Contribution Margin		$4.00
	Fixed Cost		$10,000
	Breakeven Point in Units		2,500
	Breakeven Point in Dollars		$30,000

DATA TO BE GRAPHED:

Units	TVC	Fixed Cost	Total Cost	Sales Rev.	Profit
0	0	10,000	10,000	0	(10,000)
1,000	8,000	10,000	18,000	12,000	(6,000)
2,000	16,000	10,000	26,000	24,000	(2,000)
3,000	24,000	10,000	34,000	36,000	2,000
4,000	32,000	10,000	42,000	48,000	6,000
5,000	40,000	10,000	50,000	60,000	10,000
6,000	48,000	10,000	58,000	72,000	14,000
7,000	56,000	10,000	66,000	84,000	18,000
8,000	64,000	10,000	74,000	96,000	22,000

33. FOREIGN CURRENCY TRANSLATION USING THE CURRENT RATE METHOD (Page 1 of 2)

IDENTIFICATION AREA:

Name:

Filename:

Date Created:

INPUT AREA:

ADJUSTED TRIAL BALANCE
In Dutch Guilders (DG)
December 31, Year 4

	Debit	Credit
Cash	20,000	
Accounts Receivable	35,000	
Inventory	105,000	
Equipment	60,000	
Accum. Dep.		20,000
Accounts Payable		35,000
Bonds Payable		50,000
Revenues		120,000
General Expenses	108,000	
Depreciation Expense	8,000	
Dividends	4,000	
Common Stock		62,000
Paid-in Capital in Excess of Par		44,000
Retained Earnings		9,000
Total	340,000	340,000

Exchange Rates:

	1 DG = $___
Current Exchange Rate	1.200
Average Exchange Rate	1.250
At July 31, Year 4	1.300
At June 30, Year 1	1.000

Other: All common stock was issued on June 30, Year 1 (i.e., 6/30/Y1).

Dividends were declared and paid on July 31, Year 4.

Translated Retained Earnings at 12/31/Y4 was: $5,500

33. FOREIGN CURRENCY TRANSLATION USING THE CURRENT RATE METHOD (Page 2 of 2)

OUTPUT AREA:

TRANSLATION FROM DUTCH GUILDERS TO DOLLARS
CURRENT RATE METHOD

		Dutch Guilders	Exchange Rates	U.S. Dollars
Debits:				
	Cash	20,000	1.200	24,000
	A/R	35,000	1.200	42,000
	Inventory	105,000	1.200	126,000
	Fixed Assets	60,000	1.200	72,000
	General Expenses	108,000	1.250	135,000
	Depreciation Exp.	8,000	1.250	10,000
	Dividends (7/31/Y4)	4,000	1.300	5,200
Total		340,000		414,200
Credits:				
	Accum. Depreciation	20,000	1.200	24,000
	A/P	35,000	1.200	42,000
	Bonds Payable	50,000	1.200	60,000
	Revenues	120,000	1.250	150,000
	Common Stock (6/30/Y1)	62,000	1.000	62,000
	Paid-in Cap. (6/30/Y1)	44,000	1.000	44,000
	Retained Earnings	9,000	n.a.	5,500
	Cum. Transl. Adjustment			26,700
Total		340,000		414,200

39. ECONOMIC IMPACT OF AN IMPORT QUOTA (Page 1 of 2)

IDENTIFICATION AREA:

Name:

Filename:

Date Created:

INPUT AREA:

Use the following equation to prepare a domestic demand curve:

$$P(QD) = 120 - 10*Q$$

Use the following equations to prepare a domestic supply and a world supply curve:

$$P(QS\text{-}d) = 20 + 10*Q$$
$$P(QS\text{-}w) = 30 + 0*Q$$

OUTPUT AREA:

A. Table of Q, P(QD), P(QS-d), and P(QS-w).

Q	P(QD)	P(QS-d)	P(QS-w)
0	120	20	30
1	110	30	30
2	100	40	30
3	90	50	30
4	80	60	30
5	70	70	30
6	60	80	30
7	50	90	30
8	40	100	30
9	30	110	30
10	20	120	30

39.   ECONOMIC IMPACT OF AN IMPORT QUOTA   (Page 2 of 2)

OUTPUT AREA CONTINUED:

B. Graph of the domestic demand curve, domestic supply curve, world
supply curve, and a vertical line at a quantity of 3 (quota = 3).

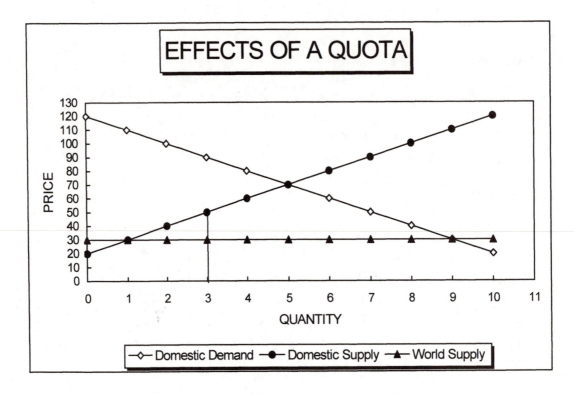

C. Equilibrium:
The world market price is $30 at any quantity demanded; in other words, the world supply curve is
perfectly elastic at a price of $30. Prior to the quota, domestic consumers could import any quantity
at a price of $30. Prior to the quoto, equilibrium price was $30 and equilibrium quantity (QD=QS)
was 9 units. As a result of the quota of 3 units, equilibrium price becomes $70 and equilibrium
quantity (QD=QS) becomes 5 units.

D. Winners and Losers:
A domestic monopolist who can persuade the government to restrict foreign competition will
benefit. The big winners in this situation are the importers who make huge profits at $70, instead
of the world market price of $30. Demoestic producers are also able to charge $70 for their output.
The losers are the domestic consumers who must pay a price of $70 rather than the world market
price of $30. If the government auctions off the right to import the good, then the profit would go to
the federal Treasury rather than the importer.

Index